Swasarnt Nerf's

Gay
Guides
for 1949

100+ Vintage Photos

With Introduction &
"Ed Leoni: a Memoir"

by Hugh Hagius

Bibliogay Publications
New York: 2010

Bibliogay Publications
P.O. Box 1008
New York, NY 10025

hughhagius@gmail.com

Revised Edition: May 2010
ISBN: 978-0-615-36024-9
This is an expanded edition of *Gay Guides for 1949* © 2004 Hugh Hagius

Printing and Distribution: lulu.com/bibliogay

Cover Illustration: *The Kiss,* snapshot made at a gay beach in the 1950s

Frontispiece: Riis Beach, 1960s

Contents

You can always stay home and curl up
with a good book

Introduction

By Hugh Hagius

Between World War II and the Korean War, the gay community was growing rapidly in numbers and in solidarity. It was a secret society invisible to the straight world; the members met in little-noticed places, recognizing each other by code words.

These guides give us a tour through that erotically charged alternate reality. The first two guides—one for New York, and one for the U.S.—were produced in 1949, and distributed through a network of friends. The readers then passed back their own discoveries through the same network for inclusion in second editions in 1950. Finally in the mid-50s a third edition of the national guide—expanded to worldwide—rolled off the mimeograph machine.

The two guides of 1949 were **SODOM-ON-HUDSON**, "Everything from the Plaza to the Pissoirs," in 28 pages, and the 69-page **The GAY GIRL'S GUIDE**, "A Primer for Novices, A Review for Roués", covering all America. If that title confuses you, consult the Gayese-English Dictionary:

> **GIRL:As a vocative, synonymous with DARLING. Also used loosely by homosexuals with reference to themselves and their friends.**

We are here in a world of **AUNTIES** and **BELLES** and **QUEENS** and **TRADE**, the gay underground of 1949.

It was an underground in deep cover. The booklets were disguised in an envelope "with a sender's identification designed to dull almost anybody's curiosity," and in the preface to the 1950 edition of **The GAY GIRL'S GUIDE** the reader is warned:

> **Be careful who you show it to. A wrong decision would have unfortunate results not only for you but for a few million others besides.**

Always rumbling in the background was war. The closing note to the 1950 edition says:

> The authors are not at present certain as to whether there will be future editions. The possibility of a new War, although it may bring a great increase of activity and many changes (which would justify a new edition), might also affect the lives of the authors in such a way as to make another impossible.

But as it turned out, the authors did produce a third edition, dated not with a year, but just as "Mid-50s," with the impressive title **Gay Girl's Guide to the U.S. & the Western World.** Not only did it have sections on French and German gayese, it had a page of phrases to help you fraternize with the enemy:

Russian Sentences

Since war with Russia remains a potential-
ity for many years, the following are
included for use if you become a P.O.W.
and have an appropriate lieutenant or
sergeant of the camp guards to practice
on. Or in the event of total victory &
occupation they may be used on chocolate-
loving boys who haven't yet learned English

I'd like to suck your cock:
Yah ho-TYEL-booey poso-SART varsh KOO-oy.

Have you got a hard-on yet?:
Yest lee oo vars ooshay soo-cuss-TOY?

What a horsecock you have:
Kar-KOY morsho-BOO-oy KOO-oy oo vars!

I sure like your cock and balls but you
   need a bath:
Mnyoh O-chen NRAV-yar-tsar varshoo MOO-dee
   no vahm NOOGE-no BARN-yar.

So long! Tomorrow night, here again?
Vsyeh-VO. ZARV-tra VYE-ch'rum, zdyays
o-PYART?

(18)

Very funny to you and me, but not calculated to amuse **LILY LAW.**

The authors' prediction of a great increase in activity in the new war did in fact happen; and with it came a heightened awareness and political consciousness in the gay community. These guides give a breaking-news report of these developments. In 1949 the only things listed were the bars and the baths and other cruising places. In the mid-50s edition, the editors instructed their readers how to find ONE magazine or get in touch with the Mattachine Society, or purchase pictures from the Athletic Model Guild. The gay community was building political and cultural institutions.

More Than Just Listings

So far as I know, these are the earliest gay guides; the Damron guides did not begin publication until 1964. And the **GAY GIRL** guides are more than just listings. They contain groundbreaking reports and essays, such as the first glossary of gay slang, the first manual of gay sex techniques, the first treatise on V.D. for gay men, and the first gay bibliography.

All this is told in the tough, unsentimental voice of a **MOTHER** teaching her dear **DAUGHTER** "to develop all her talents and get the most out of life". **MOTHER** does not mince words—words, that is, like **faggot, cock-sucking**, and **T-room**. Despite her own choice of vocabulary she insists:

> **GAY: Homosexual, queer (adj.). The only word used by homosexuals with reference to themselves, their friends their haunts, etc.**

This meaning was only for those in the know. The guide suggests that in a strange city you might ask a cabdriver to take you to "the gayest bar in town", and adds, "Whether it works depends on both the knowledge and understanding of the cabbie."

A **MOTHER's** guidance was a great help to the innocent young **GAY GIRL**, because her path was strewn with perils. She had to make her way between **DIRT** and **LILY LAW**, and cope with a world in which bars were forever being raided, and whole cities were subjected to witch-hunts—see the section on "Gay Life on the U.S.A." where the Great Purges—Madison in 1945, Los Angeles in 1946, and Chicago in 1949—are discussed.

Sex Techniques

The 17-page chapter on sex techniques is a regular kama sutra. The opinions are bold and original: "Cocksucking talent is directly proportional to age"; the taste of semen "will vary surprisingly from person to person, sometimes very mild, sometimes very tangy"; "of pairs that have been going steadily and faithfully for more than a month, 50% employ a mutual masturbation variant, 40% a 'browning combination,' and only 10% oral."

Eight pages are devoted to oral technique alone. This occasioned a spirited controversy in Gershon Legman's *Oragenitalism: Oral Techniques in Genital Excitation* (New York: Julian Press, 1969). I have a brief account of it in the following communication from Ed Leoni:

"This 1ˢᵗ is the one quoted extensively, and disparagingly, re irrumation vs fellation comments by Legman in *Oragenitalism*."

I regret that I am unable to provide any additional information on these disparaging remarks; although the New York Public Library does catalog *Oragenitalism* (under the subject *oral sex*), unfortunately it lists the volume's status as MISSING.

The sex techniques section is basically theoretical. For practical application, check the New York Guide's sections on the YMCA, the Dunes, and Everard's Baths (the Fellatorium).

Dear reader, be advised: If you decide to attempt the "rare and idyllic" oral-anal position, requiring "a great amount of contortionist prowess on the part of both partners" it is entirely at your own risk and we take no responsibility for injuries.

Who Was Swasarnt Nerf?

Several authors are credited on the title pages of the various guides, but the main one, listed in all editions, is Swasarnt Nerf. His collaborators are Mona Moosedike, Peter Asti, Daphne Dilldock, Moira Moussedaique and P. Doe Maniak.

The identity of Swasarnt Nerf (= Soixante-Neuf, Sixty-Nine) must be forever a mystery. I have a hunch that the real author concealed by this pen name is Edgar Leoni, but it is only a hunch. Ed is not widely known as a pioneer in gay studies, so I discuss his contributions in a brief memoir which follows this introduction.

It was in any case from Ed's hands that I received the five little booklets that have been reprinted here. They were mimeographed on paper trimmed to pages of 5 by 6 inches and stapled in blotter paper covers. The two first editions of 1949 are bound in purple. The two second editions of 1950 are in red. The single third edition of the mid-50s is in blue.

Mimeograph was an extremely low-tech method of printing. You had to type a stencil and affix it to a drum, add strong-smelling mimeograph fluid, and roll the drum with a hand crank. It left purple, smeary blotches on the paper and all over you too. The stencil wore out quickly and the impression became blurrier and blurrier. You got only a few dozen good copies.

So the original guides would have been produced in tiny editions—so small that Swasarnt Nerf gives his own phone number, RUddy 1-4692.

When John Loughery consulted them as part of his extensive research for writing *The Other Side of Silence*, he said, "I've heard about things like these, but these are the first I've seen." In his book John said:

> **"The 1949 *Gay Girl's Guide*, a limited edition, privately printed "networking" booklet with construction-paper covers (subtitled "A Primer for Novices, A Review for Roués"), gave lengthy descriptions of the social possibilities in New York City that year, but also compiled a list of gay bars and known cruising spots, often in hotel bars, in more than thirty other cities from Boston to San Diego. The anonymous editors requested feedback from their readers, and the 1950 edition of the *Guide* offered updates and new suggestions in cities such as Atlanta, Hartford, Omaha, Pittsburgh, and Louisville and Lexington, Kentucky."**

When you consider how fragile the little books were, and how dangerous to own, it is not likely that many have survived. The ONE Institute catalogs the two 1949 guides and the mid-50s guide, but does not list the second editions of 1950. So far as I know, the set I purchased from Ed is the only surviving complete run of the series.

The Reprint

For the reprint, I have re-keyed the originals because they were too faint or splotchy to scan. I made them resemble the original pages the best I could, with the original page numbers, and a `Courier Bold` typeface to suggest typewriting.

The two guides of 1949 are reproduced in full, because they were the most amusing and spontaneous and historically interesting.

For the editions of 1950 and the mid-50s, Swasarnt Nerf basically recycled the 1949 editions, dropping or condensing earlier parts in order to incorporate added material. I have not reprinted these editions in full, but only the new sections. The 1950 guide lists more cities than the 1949 guide does, and the mid-50s lists even more—88 cities, by my count—so I have included that list, as the latest and longest.

The Photographs

The illustrations for this reprint were given to me by my friend Richard P., a veteran of the Battle of Guadalcanal. Richard contracted dengue fever in the South Pacific, and after the War he spent some time in Veterans hospitals. When he recovered his health he did not go home to Ohio, but instead made a beeline for New York, where he spent the rest of his days.

Richard was an amateur photographer with an eye for good-looking men. He gave me a packet of snapshots with the note "GAY BEACHES, PT LOOKOUT, RIIS MOSTLY, CONEY ET AL". One of the Point Lookout pictures is dated 7-28-48, the year before the Gay Guides were published.

Most of the pictures are at the beach, but some show scenes in the city. To the untutored viewer they represent nothing but groups of men walking about and chatting— but the discerning gay eye sees heavy-duty cruising.

Besides these early pictures, there were many photographs from the gay sections of Coney Island and Atlantic City in the 1950s. In the 'sixties when the gay section Riis Beach in Queens went nude, Richard P. was there with his camera. You do not need special powers to see that these are gay crowds.

Those happy days at Riis Beach lasted until 1972 when the National Park Service took over and the rangers started giving tickets to the unclad.

The other packet contained pornography, including a Sepia-print photo and a few Polaroids, as well as some studio prints and also some contact prints and enlargements, several with cropping marks. None of them has a photographer's stamp or signature, or any information to date them, but they seem to range from the '40s to the early '70s.

I have laid out the earlier snapshots along with the text of the gay guides, in chronological order as best I could guess it. The Riis Beach snapshots, a little pornography, and the physique magazine covers appear separately in Photo Essays.

The Lady Jai Recommended List

As I was writing an earliler version of this introduction in 2003, I got a note from Tim Retzloff of the University of Michigan. Tim is the author of "Cars and Bars," the history of how the automobile liberated gay men in postwar Flint, Mich.

He kindly sent me a copy of another mimeographed bar list which used to circulate around Detroit, compiled by a person using the nom de plume Lady Jai. Lady Jai's list is reprinted at the end of this volume.

6

Edgar H. Leoni (1925-1996): A Memoir

By Hugh Hagius

I was not really surprised when I thumbed through *The Crimson Letter*, Douglass Shand-Tucci's history of Homosexual Harvard, and found no mention of Edgar Hugh Leoni.   Ed was one of Harvard's queerest sons (B.A., Class of 1945), but he operated so deep underground that he missed much of the recognition he deserves as a trailblazer for the study of gay history.

Ed Leoni

This is so partly because he published his gay researches under pen names, and partly because his main contribution to gay studies was a necessary but unglamorous bibliography. In that little book, he published the real names of the authors of more than a dozen gay works published under pseudonyms, so now it is only fair to do the same for him.

I met Ed in 1982, when I was looking for a copy of the Noel I. Garde bibliography, *The Homosexual in Literature*. I asked C.J. Scheiner where it was to be found, and he referred me to Ed Leoni. I asked C.J., "Do you know anything about Noel I. Garde?" and C.J. said, "All I know is, Noel I. Garde has the same letters in his name as Edgar Leoni, and Leoni always has brand-new copies of his books."

When I called Ed, I asked him about Noel I. Garde. He was vague and evasive, so I decided to try a trick. I sent a check for the bibliography and enclosed a note asking Ed to autograph the copy. He replied with this firm non-denial:

"Sorry, but I can't see where you could anticipate any chances of autographing…The Garde biblio, while a fine copy, is not autographed. I have never come across any autographed Garde copy. Your request recalls similar from Scheiner and sounds like replay. I hope that otherwise you will be pleased."

So Ed would not acknowledge—at least to me or to C.J.—that he was Noel I. Garde. That would have been too easy. Of course the anagram is a tip-off, and the ONE Archives now officially identify Ed as the author of the Garde books.

But in some quarters, it is still a secret. The big gay bibliographies list Noel I. Garde only, and do not mention Edgar Leoni (who was not a gay writer). And the Library of Congress and the New York Public Library are both clueless. They catalog the two names separately, with no indication that Noel I. Garde is a pseudonym.

Ed's secrecy, I think, was part of the caution routinely practiced in the gay world in his generation; and he also needed to keep the persona of Noel I. Garde distinct from the Edgar Leoni who published **Nostradamus and His Prophecies**, his blockbuster.

But I believe the real reason he was so mysterious was that it would have ruined the fun to give the game away by just admitting authorship. Ed loved literary sleuthing, especially the discovery of secret identities. I shared this quirky interest, and it gave us a lot to talk about.

After the bibliography, I bought more books from Ed, including Noel I. Garde's **Jonathan to Gide**, as well as other hard-to-get items. When I got **Nostradamus**, he kindly inscribed it for me (as Edgar Leoni, of course).

We usually kept in touch through letters, even though we lived only a few blocks apart. In 1992 he sent me a note saying he was moving to Florida and selling all his books, a whole apartment full. They included a complete run of **The GAY GIRL'S GUIDES**, the dishy little books reprinted in this volume. Ed took a special interest in these guides and I could tell he wanted them to have a good home; and I knew I was lucky to get them.

At the same time he gave me a bundle of his own miscellaneous papers. They were very miscellaneous indeed—letters and articles and translations, things he had copied out from other publications, notes for research, and even detailed records of some of his dreams.

These items are on my desk—the two Noel I. Garde books, **Nostradamus**, **The GAY GIRL'S GUIDES**, his letters to me, and the miscellaneous papers—as I write this memorandum of Ed's literary productions.

1. Swasarnt Nerf Guides (1949 to mid-fifties)

As soon as I had a good look at the **The GAY GIRL'S GUIDES**, I could see many of Ed's distinctive touches, enough to convince me that he had a hand in producing them.

There is no proof, but there are plenty of clues. Nerf exhibits Ed's trademark combination of hardboiled diction and fussy grammar—for example, Nerf (correctly) uses *penes* as the plural of *penis*. The most telling evidence is this: The guides include bibliography sections, which from edition to edition grow more elaborate and scientific, gradually morphing into a prototype of the Noel I. Garde bibliography.

These booklets began publication two years after Ed's graduation from Harvard in 1947. The *Harvard Alumni Directory* says his B.A. degree was conferred in 1947, as a member of the Class of 1945, but does not explain the delay. I expect it had something to do with the draft.

Ed departed Harvard with a solid classical foundation and a good command of Latin and French. Soon after that, he must have been vigorously pursuing queer researches in New York, because **The GAY GIRL'S GUIDES** are crammed with information collected in the field.

The national editions of these pamphlets contain bibliographies. You could count Kinsey (1948) as the first bibliography on homosexuality, but for myself, I think the **GAY GIRL'S GUIDE** is the first really <u>gay</u> bibliography, and it has terrific thumbnail reviews like these:

> ***The Sling and the Arrow*** **(1947): A middle-aged businessman gets queerer and queerer, sends his wife off to the office, gets all upset by a sailor and ends up being chased around town in drag by the police.**

> ***The Fall of Valor*** **(1947): Prof. falls in love with the other husband and thinks he is getting somewhere until bashed on the head.**

> **Thomas Mann's *Death in Venice*: While this may be tops in literary value, it is a rather dull story about an old man drooling over a little Polish bitch.**

In later editions the entries become briefer, more numerous, and more like the eventual Noel I. Garde bibliography.

2. Noel I. Garde: Periodical Articles (1958-1960)

Ed contributed a number of articles for ONE as Noel I. Garde.

Here I am able to specify only the articles revealing the identity of Xavier Mayne as Edward Irenaeus Prime-Stevenson:

> **"The Mysterious Father of American Homophile Literature" (ONE INSTITUTE QUARTERLY, No. 3, Fall 1958) and "The First Native American 'Gay' Novel" (ONE INSTITUTE QUARTERLY, No. 9, Spring 1960).** (Burton Weiss Catalog Inventory No. 18075).

Cracking this secret must have been catnip to Ed.

Burton Weiss also informs us that Ed furnished the copy of Xavier Mayne's *The Intersexes* which was used for the Arno facsimile reprint in 1975.

Another may be an article written during the 1960 Presidential Campaign. A carbon copy duplicate is among the papers Ed gave me. The article starts by mentioning the sensation caused by Alan Drury's novel **Advise and Consent**, and recalls a similar sensation in real life, the 1942 scandal involving Senator David I. Walsh of Massachusetts, chairman of the Senate Naval Affairs Committee. The article says:

> **"It was charged that as a regular patron of a recently-raided house of male prostitution located in Pacific Street, Brooklyn, the Senator had taken his Naval Affairs duties so conscientiously that he felt impelled to give his personal attention to the hard problems of various sailors."**

The FBI suspected that the entrepreneur who was recruiting sailors for this establishment was a Nazi agent.

3. Noel I. Garde: The Homosexual in Literature (1959)

Gay bibliography was a passion with Ed, and he worked on it all his life. It started with brief notices of gay-themed books in the 1949 GAY GIRL'S GUIDE, which eventually became **The Homosexual in Literature**, published in 1959. After that he continued to compile listings, producing a supplement, which he called **The Checklist** and distributed to his friends; and a large catalog of the volumes in his 1992 relocation sale. His letters are filled with bibliographical minutiae.

Secret Identities Revealed

These are the pseudonyms and the real authors Edgar Leoni identified in the Noel I. Garde bibliography, **The Homosexual in Literature**. A question mark indicates a conjecture.

Pseudonym	Title	Real Author
	Don Leon	George Colman, Jr.?
Alan Dale	A Marriage Below Zero	Alfred J. Cohen
Camille des Grieux	Teleny	Oscar Wilde?
		Lord Alfred Douglas?
John Francis Bloxham	The Priest and the Acolyte	Lord Alfred Douglas?
Xavier Mayne	Imre: a Memorandum	Edward I. Prime-Stevenson
Grace Z. Stone	The Grotto	Ethel Vance
Rodney Garland	The Heart in Exile	Adam de Hegedus
George Taylor	Antinous	Adolph Hausrath
Christopher Carr	Memoirs of Arthur Hamilton	Arthur C. Benson
Frederick Baron Corvo	In His Own Image	Frederick Rolfe
Lord Stites	Intimate Acrobatica	Donald Fairchild
Matthew Head	The Smell of Money	John E. Canaday
Stuart Benton	All Things Human	George Sylvester Viereck
Edgar Box	Death in the Fifth Position	Gore Vidal

The 1959 publication was 32 pages long and was printed by the Village Press, one of Ed's own imprints. It listed more than 600 items, and was restricted to "literature," meaning novels, poems, short stories, and plays. It also was restricted to publications in English, and in book form. Finally, "The Homosexual" of the title meant only gay men, not lesbians.

Even with these limitations, it was an important contribution, and Arno Press reprinted it in 1975 in its series of fundamental documents of the homophile movement.

It is easy to forget how hard it was in 1959 to find information about homosexuality. A bibliography is a powerful tool. Without one, every single reader had to start from scratch, plowing through all of literature looking for the parts that make your pulse race. The gay classics had to be rediscovered again and again.

We now have a number of big, first-rate bibliographies, such as the works of Young, Bullough, Dynes, and Weinberg & Bell, which have superseded *The Homosexual in Literature*. But bibliography is a cumulative science; later scholars build upon the lists compiled by those who worked before them, and those huge tomes list Ed's modest little pamphlet, and include the books he listed. When Young says, "I remain indebted to the compilers of several previous lists," the first one he mentions is Noel I. Garde.

> The Homosexual
> In Literature
>
> A Chronological Bibliography
> Circa 700 B. C. - 1958
> By Noel I. Garde

In his bibliography, Ed also took the opportunity to publish the real names for eleven pseudonyms, and conjectures for three others (see table opposite page).

4. Edgar Leoni: Nostradamus and His Prophecies (1961)

Nostradamus: Life and Literature was published in 1961 by Nosbooks, another of Ed's own imprints. The title was changed in later editions to *Nostradamus and His Prophecies*.

For readers unacquainted with the occult sciences, I will mention that Michel Nostradamus (1503-1566) was the court astrologer to Queen Marie de' Medici of France. His horoscopes murkily foretold the calamities fated for that unfortunate queen's doomed children. He also produced predictions of the future in the form of verse quatrains, which were published in groups of 100 called centuries. They run the entire range from cryptic to enigmatic, sometimes soaring to the incomprehensible.

Nostradamus is a magnet for crackpots, but Ed was not a crackpot. He identified an audience of readers starved for information on a topic no academic scholar dared to touch.

Ed's introduction begins, "The purpose of this book is to provide *everything* by and about Nostradamus," and it delivers. He produced a critical edition of the centuries displaying the original text on the left and his own translation on facing pages. He added a biography, an annotated bibliography, 19 plates, a background essay, a commentary upon the verses, many indexes, genealogy charts of the Valois, Lorraine, Burgundy, Bourbon and Habsburg families, lists of dubious words, a chronology, an astrological chart, and even the forgeries.

All this took more than eleven years to do. The New York Public Library catalog lists a typescript by Edgar Leoni titled **Michel Nostradamus: life and works**, which must have been the earliest version. I suppose this was a gift of Ed's to the library; unfortunately it is now listed as MISSING. CATNYP says it was 1027 pages bound in three volumes, and dates it as 1950, so Ed must have started to work on Nostradamus in the '40s, not long after graduating from Harvard.

He published it himself, just as he did with the guides and the bibliography. The first printing was done by Exposition Press, a subsidy publisher, and on some copies he pasted Nosbooks imprint stickers over the Exposition logo.

After writing the book and publishing it, Ed next set about to promote it. The distinguished historian Crane Brinton (of Harvard, natch) gave it a favorable notice in **The American Historical Review**—"meticulous scholarship...surprisingly interesting reading".

Ed sent letters to every public library in the country, advising the librarians that at last they could offer a respectable book to the many patrons who inquired about Nostradamus. (The alignment of the stars for library acquisitions has not, however, always been favorable. The New York Public Library catalogs all its copies as MISSING, and the Library of Congress lists its Leoni holdings as LOST.)

Soon the book was selling. Ed retained the copyright, so he was able to take it to big commercial publishers and dictate terms. My copy is the 1982 edition and it says, "Copyright © MCMLXI by Edgar Leoni All rights reserved. This 1982 edition is published by Bell Publishing Company, distributed by Crown Publishers, Inc., by arrangement with Edgar Leoni." It is now published by Dover, 822 pages, list price $19.95 and it sells steadily.

To give you an idea of the book, this is the first prophecy, Quatrain 1 of Century I:

> **"Being seated by night in secret study,**
> **Alone resting on the brass stool:**
> **A slight flame coming forth from the solitude**
> **That which is not believed in vain is made to succeed."**

As you can see, Nostradamus very accurately predicted the fate of Ed's book!

5. Noel I. Garde: Jonathan to Gide (1964)

Noel I. Garde struck again in 1964, with the publication of *Jonathan to Gide: the Homosexual in History,* a gay Who's Who. This book weighed in at 751 pages with three indexes and a bibliography, and it outs 300 great or famous men rumored or known to be gay, giving brief biographical sketches of each. These include the obvious ones, but also some surprises: Jesus, Richard the Lion-Hearted, George Washington, Napoleon, Wild Bill Hickok.

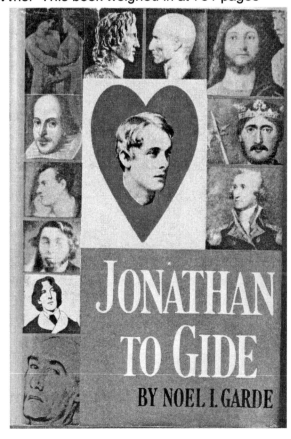

Ed published it himself, of course. In some copies he pasted the Nosbooks label over the logo of the subsidy publisher Vantage Press. My copy, purchased from Ed, has only the Vantage logo and lacks the Nosbooks label.

This book is entertaining and interesting, but it is not a scholarly work. Wayne Dynes tactfully remarks, "Based on secondary sources, this book must be used with caution." And it has some mistakes. Ed knew about some of these, because they were pointed out to him, sometimes by critical reviews or comments.

Ed suspected some critics of helping themselves to his work without giving him credit. When they copied one of his mistakes, he had them nailed. He caught one in flagrante delicto, a certain G.W. who wrote in The Guild Bulletin #20. One of Ed's papers denounces G.W.'s larceny and it bears the title: "How to Plagiarize While Sneering, by G.W."

Despite its flaws, the book is useful because of its enormous breadth and unsparing dishiness. No other book of its kind has such scope, with tales of caliphs, sultans, generals, czars, and scientists, the fruit of Ed's omnivorous reading. *Jonathan to Gide* is fun and informative, and gives full references, so the interested reader can consult Ed's own sources. If you quote it without checking, you risk repeating a mistake; but if you don't use it at all, you risk missing some out-of-the-way information you are not likely to find anywhere else.

Revising and Marketing

After these great labors, silence. As far as I know, Ed did not publish any more books.

In the five years from 1959 to 1964, he produced the bibliography, *Nostradamus*, and *Jonathan to Gide*, and he did it all—he wrote the books, he edited the books, he sent the copy to the printers (the guides and bibliography he typed himself), he read the proofs, he published the books, he promoted the books, and he sold the books.

I think after 1964 his main energies were devoted to the selling, and especially the revising and marketing of *Nostradamus and His Prophecies* through several editions. He watched the book's sales very carefully, even at the level of individual bookstores. When I wanted to buy it, he told me which copy to select, on which shelf, at which bookstore. I gathered from some offhand remarks that he was a very tough bargainer with Bell and he had many indignant discussions with Crown about advertising and distribution.

Even so, he did not stop his researches as a literary detective. His projects during the 1980s included investigating such questions as, Was Lord Alfred Douglas the author of *Teleny*? Was Jack the Ripper really the Prince of Wales? At the time I was developing an argument that the Robert Scully who wrote *A Scarlet Pansy* was really Robert McAlmon, so we swapped secret-identity theories.

These preoccupations even invaded his dream life. One of the dreams included among the sheaf of miscellaneous papers is headed "A Strange Gay-Porno-Biblio Dream by EHL." In the dream Ed is at a combination convention-and-sales-meeting of gay porno publishers in a hotel ballroom, where he has the opportunity to meet the porn writer Rich Cummings.

The dream continues:

> "When I saw the person who was obviously intended as such, he was a sort of fading ex-young-doll-possibly-callboy, medium build, fair, nice features (of well-known people, Mickey Rooney would be closest I can think of, but somewhat better looking), about 26-28. He was much fussed over, presumably by queens (no faces remembered) and clearly following instructions to be nice and polite to everyone. Since I knew of course that "Cummings" aka Samuel West aka Jason Forbes was a middle-aged Bronx Jew, I was of course outraged at the fraud..."

At the end of the dream Ed exposes the fraudulent porn author as a Los Angeles call boy.

The Leoni Archives

In 1997 John Loughery was doing research for *The Other Side of Silence,* his monumental history of gay America. Before setting off on pilgrimage to the venerable shrines of gay life across the land, he consulted the listings in The GAY GIRL'S GUIDES. At that time I suggested that he would find Ed a rich source of information. But before John could contact Ed, he read in the ONE Institute newsletter that Ed had died.

ONE said that Lyle Henry and John O'Brien recently had made a sweep of the South, searching for material for the institute's archives. In Tampa they learned that Ed had died the previous year. The newsletter continues:

> "After discussions with his estate attorney in Tampa, ONE Institute learned that Leoni's niece and her husband had cleared out his house and storage area. They had taken everything from Tampa back to their own home in Arkansas. After a search for the materials through a series of letters and phone calls, Leoni's family agreed to turn over to ONE his promised books, photos, cards and diaries. It cannot be understated that had the workers from ONE not arrived in Arkansas when they did the collection would have been lost. The niece had planned to throw it out that very night (but not the thousands she inherited!)"

These materials now are catalogued in the ONE National Gay and Lesbian Archives in Los Angeles—three feet of materials in six cartons and one shoebox.

Among the items retrieved was Ed's diary in 17 volumes, beginning in 1935, when he was only nine years old. Beginning in 1939, when he turned 13, the diaries are locked.

The ONE archivist, Michael P. Palmer, also provides some biographical details—that Ed earned a master's degree at Columbia University and that he was employed in the insurance industry. Palmer does not say in what capacity, or give other details. Probably much more information about his life awaits the researcher who sifts through those three feet of material, especially the locked diaries.

But with what we do know, I think Ed's citizenship in the Gay Republic of Letters is secure. The bibliography, *Jonathan to Gide* and *Nostradamus* are all honorable contributions to scholarship. And **The GAY GIRL'S GUIDES** are still fresh and sassy and alive.

Nostradamus and His Prophecies is of course Ed's chief work—superseded for scholarly work, but still selling briskly and in copyright until 2046, thanks to the Sonny Bono Law. In the wave of national anxiety that followed the Sept. attacks of Sept. 11, 2001, its sales peaked, and for a short time it appeared in the Advice, How-to and Miscellaneous section of the New York Times' Best Sellers List.

And here are a few last words from Ed—some translations which were among the papers he gave to me.

Verses from *The Priapeia*

Translated by Edgar Leoni

(Among Ed's papers was a selection of translations from **The Priapeia**, *the collection of inscriptions affixed to the statues of Priapus which the Romans put in orchards and gardens to ward off thieves. Here are some of them.—HH)*

Song #10: Priapus

Be warned not to steal: I will seize you, but 'tis not with a cudgel you will get it:
I will give you fierce wounds with my uncurved scythe.
You will be pierced by my own foot-long tool,
So that you will think your ass had no grooves.

Song #12: Priapus

I warn boys with threats of being browned, girls of getting fucked:
For the mature thief, a third punishment remains.

Song #24: Priapus

This sceptre, that which after it is cut off from a tree,
Has never yet been able to survive in any yard;
The sceptre, which browning-queens ("pathic girls") seek;
Which kings desire to have in them;
To which noble cock-suckers give kisses;
It goes into the guts of the thief, right up to the
Pubes and cock and balls.

Gaedicker's

SODOM-ON-HUDSON

Spring, 1949

Gaedicker's

SODOM-ON-HUDSON

("Everything from the Plaza
                    to the Pissoirs"

Prepared in cooperation with the
Sodomite Chamber of Commerce, the
Sothamite Tourist Bureau and the
Gomorran Geodetic Survey. Under
the general editorial supervision
of Swasarnt Nerf of the American
Fellatelic Society, with the assist-
ance of Mona Moosedike of the
Canadian Clitorical Committee

Endorsed by the N.A.Q.

Spring, 1949

Gaedicker's

SODOM-ON-HUDSON

("Everything from the Plaza
                    to the Pissoirs")

Prepared in cooperation with the
Sodomite Chamber of Commerce, the
Sothamite Tourist Bureau, and the
Gomorrah Geodetic Survey. Under
the general editorial supervision
of Swasarnt Nerf of the American
Fellatelic Society, with the assist-
ance of Mona Moosedike of the
Canadian Clitorical Committee.

Endorsed by the N.A.Q.

Spring, 1949

New York is the World Capital of Government, Finance, Drama, Publishing, and last, but far from least, of Faggotry.

No other city, in the United States or in the World, can boast of as large and as continually-varying a collection of faggots as New York. And little wonder: however much its fixed population may vary, New York continues to be the Mecca of Meccas for every faggot from Massachusetts to Mexico and from Norway to New Zealand.

New York has a most abundant supply of all varieties of faggotic background, so abundant as to dwarf equivalent areas in any rival city inhabited by Man.

THE OUTDOORS

Doubtless, the best insurance of New York's eternal strength lies in its vast and far-flung assortment of outdoor cruising areas, which can be considered impervious to any conceivable amount of "heat", even if such a condition could be associated with the N.Y.P.D.

(1)

Hanging Out in Central Park

Working our way upwards, let us first consider Bryant
Park at 42nd St. & Sixth Avenue. While there is some
representation in all parts of this small park, the
heaviest concentration lies along the raised promenade at the
eastern extremity. For the most part, the habitués are
professional and semi-professional—some, let it be noted, of
the highest pulchritudinous level. Here in warm seasons, we
find a sort of union headquarters, or even hiring hall, with
the most friendly camaraderie between the roughest of trade
and the swishiest of faggots. In addition, however, a
substantial amount of amateur talent drops into this area
frequently, in view of its strategic location in the heart of
New York, the scene of so many attractions. In short, there
is really everything to be found in Bryant Park sooner or
later.

Moving uptown, our next major area is Rockefeller
Plaza. The main drag here is on the western side, though
some activity is spread around the entire plaza. On the
whole, the class of habitués is relatively genteel. Like
Bryant Park,

(2)

activity is pretty well limited to the warm seasons; in
winter, the place is overrun by an invasion of
heterosexual barbarians watching the ice skating below (in
which, by the way, many faggots participate too).

We now move toward the third and greatest area, Central
Park. Between Rockefeller Center and the Park, the most popular
route lies along Fifth Avenue. A large number of queens are to
be seen thereon, between 50th and 59th Sts., especially on the
western side, and in better weather.

While it is often claimed that there is something going on
everywhere in the Park, there are actually but two main areas
(and some minor ones) between W. 79th St. and E. 59th St.

The lower of the two main areas is in the vicinity of a
body of water called The Pond, and is popularly known by the ill-
conceived name of Vaseline Alley. Its form is that of a 9 (or if
you insist on

(3)

being filthy, girl, make your own comparison). The tip of the
9's stem is at 59th and Fifth, along the path on the west side
of the East Drive. In the summer, the benches will be found
crowded, more faggotically as we parallel 62nd St. At a point
abreast of 64th St. we find a downward path to the left, and a
bridge. The circular part of the 9 is the area around the Pond
north of this bridge (though at times there may be activity
anywhere along the periphery of the entire Pond). If we keep
bearing to the right, we complete a circle and come back to the
original path. The heaviest concentration is found between the
bridge and a junction of five paths a hundred odd yards beyond.
But just beyond the bridge, we find steps down to a walk along
the Pond, which is often heavily populated. Between the walk
and the upper path lies a substantial amount of rocky and bushy
terrain, and here a considerable bit of activity goes on at
times to show just how inapt is the name of Vaseline Alley (in
comparison with, say, Saliva Street).

(4)

Vaseline Alley has the advantage of being the scene of activity
all year around, which is true of few other outdoor places. It
is also frequented by everyone, from the lowly sluts to a
certain well-known star of stage and screen, whose initials are
FT. It is also one of the best places in New York for non-
professional chicken. It has the disadvantage, however, of
being the scene of periodic tours by the cars, motorcycles and
flat feet of New York's finest.

If, instead of turning downward to the left, we continue
along the western side of the East Drive, we are on our way to
the second major area in the Park, "The Forest". We cross the
Transverse Road and proceed along to the Mall, then under a
traffic bridge (at this point headqueens may wish to make a
detour: we find it on our left as we start to go under the
bridge). We have now come to the Lake. In the summer, there
may be something to be found in the area we have just traversed,
especially in the vicinity of the Mall where there are then
concerts.

(5)

The Lake is roughly in the form of a right angle, with one part going north-south and the other part east-west. Between these two arms is the area aptly known as "The Forest", consisting of small, winding paths with a severe grade, amidst heavy foliage, rocks and sheer drops. The heaviest concentration lies in the northwestern part, approximately abreast of 79th St., on the edge of the Forest, overlooking several bridges. Being both so far "inland" and so full of dangerous terrain, this area is popular only in good weather (unlike Vaseline Alley).

If we bear west from the northern-most part of this area, going downhill again and crossing the West Drive, we come to a minor cruising area, abreast of 79th St. and dominated by a bridge going over an insignificant and shallow arm of the Lake. This is right near the western edge of the Park and Central Park West. From this exit on CPW (79th St.) down to Columbus Circle, the benches on the eastern side of CPW are likely to

(6)

Central Park, The Rambles

have something worth noting here and there. There is another entrance to the Park at 69th St. When bearing to the right here, we come to a children's playground, approximately abreast of 67th St., the environs of which forms yet another Central Park cruising ground.

It will be noted that the main axis of cruising in the Park runs like a diagonal from southeast to northwest. Generally speaking, 80th St. can be considered the northern limits for cruising in the Park, the huge Reservoir and very open country coming soon after.

The fourth and last major area is the Riverside Park locale. It begins where Riverside Drive does, at 72nd St. Between there and 79th St., we find a twin lane below the Drive, of which the eastern one is somewhat darker and more popular. At 79th St., the promenade is interrupted by a cross street. The heaviest concentration still follows through the Park, north of this intersection, to about 85th St. At this

(7)

point, it is advisable to take the path up to the Drive, since the park becomes too open to be practicable. At 87th St. we find a very popular "lookout" edifice, and at 89th St. the heart of the area, the Soldiers and Sailors Monument, an apt enough cruising ground.

Such are the major outdoor areas. In addition, there are minor parks, such as Ft. Washington near the George Washington Bridge (for Heights queens) and Washington Square in the Village. There are whole blocks, like 42nd between 7th & 8th Aves. (once aptly called "The Meat Market") or Sixth Ave. between 40th & 42nd Sts., and whole sections of avenues like Fifth in the fifties and Lexington from about 45th to 57th. And there are intersections like 42nd & Bway (NW), 42nd & 8th (NE), Sixth Ave. & 8th St., Columbus Circle et al. Most things found in these areas are often commercially tinged.

Before leaving the outdoor field, mention must be made of the Financial District. Visitors to New York City who may become

(8)

Central Park West, Opposite the Dakota

disappointed in the general pulchritudinous level of New Yorkers
will have their opinion changed by a walk during business hours
around the downtown area, between Fulton Street and the end of
Broadway at Bowling Green. The Times Square of this area is
either Bway and Wall or Wall and Nassau. The visitor standing
for any length of time (especially during lunch hour) at either
intersection will see a fair proportion of the most beautiful
youths in New York (here for the first time we refer to Greater
New York rather than Manhattan).

There is something of a rendezvous for the Wall Street
queens in the Federal Hall Museum, located at one of the above
intersections, Wall and Nassau. They can be found on the steps
in front, or inside purportedly looking at relics of The Great
Father and most of all in the local T-room, which will be
mentioned in its proper place. But very few of these Museumites
will be found to have much similarity to the above-mentioned
dolls, as the pessimist might expect.

(9)

BARS

New York's bars are subject to a great deal of change in relative activity and popularity. Some can be considered fairly "permanent", others are here today and straight tomorrow. But once again, the number is enormous, to suit every taste.

Starting in the Village, we find the local Big Three: MacDougal's near 3rd St. and Mary's and Main Street on 8th St. (All between 5th and 6th Aves.) The character of the habitués and relative prosperity show periodic change, sometimes not always due to the NYPD, so that no comments would have very long validity, except that the Village bars are always among the livelier.

In addition to the Big Three, there are a few other bars of minor note, such as those frequented by the elegant—the Number One at 5th Ave. & 8th St. and the Little Casino at 3rd and Sullivan. Tony Pastor's, traditional GHQ for NY Lesbians and chief haunt for tourists, located on

(10)

3rd St. near Sixth Ave., has long since come to contain a collection of tourists of various sorts outnumbering the dikes and the handful of male faggots by about three to one. For the benefit of fish-queens, more dikes are likely to be found at Terry's, near MacDougal's. Mona's, a fairly new bar opposite Pastor's, has thus far failed as an imitation of its Friscan namesake, the onetime national GHQ for North American Dikes.

The East-Side bars proper extend on or near Lexington Avenue (affectionately called "Sexy-Lexy" by east-side queens) from 45th to 53rd St. At 45th east of Lexington we find the rather elegant Golden Pheasant, favorite hangout of the would-be-kept. Near 52nd on Lexington we find the small and quiet Allan's, and around the corner the remains of the once-flourishing Blue Parrot which, in spite of its beautiful layout, has not yet at this writing recovered completely from a quasi-raid and subsequent police pressure. Back again on Lexington, near 53rd we come upon the brightly-lit and repressed

(11)

Hanging Out at the Queensboro Bridge

Town Bar. In the same area, we also find some minor joints along Third Ave., more proletarian in tone, such as Sonny's at 50th St. and The Swan near 48th.

At not too great a distance, we find a cluster of piss-elegant places. On 57th east of Lexington an old favorite, Spivy's Roof, still flourishes now and then. On Lexington near 58th we find a relatively new favorite of the piss-elegant set, the Sazarac. As we move west from Lexington to Fifth, we come to two of the most elegant bars, that of the Pierre at 61st and that of the Oak Room at the Plaza on 59th. Moving further west and south, we come to yet another two bars of the elegant, the New Towne ("Town-E") on 58th west of Sixth, and Tony's on 52nd east of Sixth. Like most elegant bars, all of these are only partially gay.

All by itself on 72nd St. east of Broadway we find the New Verdi Square, with a large floor-space, many booths, and a comfortable unpretentious atmosphere. This is the favorite hangout of

(12)

the west-side queens and the lesser elegant from all over New York. It is probably the all-around nicest gaybar in New York.

Finally, in the Times Square or Midtown area, we find a multiplicity of bars of all types. The chief one, doing probably the most business of all NY gay bars, with the largest weekly turnover and with the greatest variety of patrons, is that perennial favorite, the Silver Rail (née Pink Elephant) at 43rd and 6th Ave. It is the only bar with some faggots at almost any hour of the day, any day of the week. Though often erroneously considered a low dive, its habitués run from the quite elegant (nominally "slumming") to the service-trade-and-proletariat level. It has one of the largest army and navy representations.

This is the only completely gay and major bar in the area. The rest are mixed or border-line. On 52nd between 6th and 7th Aves. are two "mixed" bars. The Ben Yee caters mostly to the lower-income show people, especially from the

(13)

Roxy. The Backstage has a fair proportion of faggots at times, some of the same type as Ben Yee. The Astor at 45th & Bway is essentially passé from its wartime glory, but now then a few more elegant queens turn up there, especially to meet out-of-town friends. Diamond Jim's at 42nd & Bway has a large proportion of servicemen, some of them trade (mostly commercial) and is frequented also by some younger civilians (also mostly commercial) and by older ones interested in either of the two foregoing. Other bars get a gay proportion now and then, the changes being due to chance police pressure or managerial moods: Crossroads (Times Square); Hurley's (45th between 7th and 8th); Gilroy's (8th Ave. between 42nd & 43rd)—at present completely defaggotized by a raid; Moss' (formerly Ross') (8th Ave. between 42nd & 43rd) and Haly's (6th Ave. between 42nd & 43$^{rd.}$).

In discussing gaybars, we have thus far approached them for the most part

(14)

by locale. If we were to consider them on a socio-psycho basis, the listing would run something like this:

Piss-Elegant: Little Casino, One Fifth
                       Avenue, Pierre, Plaza,
                       Sazarac, Spivy's Roof,
                       Tony's.
Elegant or quiet: Allan's, Blue Parrot,
                       Golden Pheasant, New
                       Towne, Town Bar
Bourgeois-Bohemian: New Verdi
All Types & Lively: MacDougals's, Main
                       Street, Mary's,
                       Silver Rail.

DRAG SHOW NIGHT CLUBS

New York boasts two all-out drag shows. The 181 (Second Avenue near 12th) is the more elegant and pretentious of the two. The 111 (East 28th near Lexington) has a somewhat more bohemian atmosphere but has almost as high a minimum. The relative quality of the shows changes periodically. Most of the patrons at both places are straight tourists, as usual. In addition, the Moroccan Village on 8th St. east of 6th has a similar show often.

(15)

An Outing at Point Lookout (Dated 7-28-48)

Point Lookout

DANCING

For homosexual dancing, there is but one real public place. Phil Black's in Harlem on 126th St. just west of 5th provides a dance floor and seating space for a fixed price of admission, with drinks optional, amidst a rather drab setting several flights up. His former lavish place, which was wont to draw some of the highest classes of the elegantsia, has long since been closed by the police (in a friendly way). The present version is principally active on Sunday evening, otherwise on occasions when a drag ball is thrown there. Much of a novel written in 1931, "Strange Brother", was set in one of his old places.

T-ROOMS

It would be very difficult to fix any complete list for head-queens. In addition to those found in many of the movies (see below), the most notorious, though hardly of any attractions, is that of Grand Central Station. Of the bars, only that of Diamond Jim's has much significance. Across the street

(16)

from the latter, that of the Chase Cafeteria is occasionally popular with the lower levels. By way of contrast, the t-room in the basement floor of the Shelton Hotel (Lexington near 49th) is quite popular with the more elegant head-queens.

Some of the subways, especially the Independent (and, in turn especially Columbus Circle (2) and Washington Sq.), have their Subway Sams.

In our discussion of the Outdoors, we have already come upon both the one near the Mall and the one in the Federal Hall Museum. The latter is quite popular during lunch-hour (between 11 and 2) for Wall Street queens, as long as the black nose of the building policeman is kept out.

What is believed to be the only surviving glory-hole, phallic size (also known as suck-hole) in any public building in New York is found at Loew's Avenue B (5th St 2 blocks east of First Avenue).

(17)

Point Lookout

Point Lookout—Drag Show

MOVIE THEATERS ETC.

New York's gay theaters are many and are subject to periodic change of conditions.

Almost all the cheaper second-run and foreign theaters in the Times Square area have a substantial amount of faggotic activity. The balconies of the Dix (last row) and of the Little Met are particularly recommended, and perhaps also the second balcony of the Lyric. For the elegant, S.R. at the Opera.

On the east side, the balcony of the Beverly (50th and 3rd Ave.) will be found the last word in tempo, if not in quality, showing many resemblances to a Turkish Bath. Some activity may also be found at the Trans-Lux Colony (79th & Second Ave.), the 68th St. Playhouse (3rd Ave.), the Grande (86th & 3rd Ave.) and the Trans-Lux Monroe (76th & 1st Ave.).

On the upper west side, the Riverside (Bway & 96th) and the Arden (103 & Columbus) also have their attractions.

(18)

Point Lookout—Drag Show

THE FELLATORIUM

Everard's Turkish Baths, incongruously occupying the site of a Greek Orthodox Church on 28th St. near Bway, plays a major role in New York's gay life.

On weekend nights, there is almost always a waiting line after 10 PM, sometimes over an hour long for dormitory space and longer yet for rooms. Most of the activity takes place in the huge dormitory on the second floor. There are some rooms around this dormitory, but most are on the third floor. Below the street level, for any who may be interested, are found the steam room, showers and even a swimming pool, the use of any of which frequently appears to arouse the indignant resentment of the attendants.

As we have mentioned, the center of gravity, even for most of those with rooms on the third floor (who upon find-ing nothing on their hallway on which to go down, come down) is the dormitory

(19)

in which the activity is such a marvel of non-inhibition as to
warm any psychoanalyst's heart. About 80% of the activity is
divided between aunties who go around groping and fellating
anyone who'll let them and responds, respectively; and
conversely, by the relatively younger faggots who maintain a
persistently passive approach to noblesse oblige (rough-trade-
à-la-reine). Only a portion of the relatively younger
remaining elements engages in any real reciprocal sexual
orgies. (The two are frequently mixed: we may find a subject
often enough engaged in kissing a contemporary in the upper
sphere while being simultaneously fellated in the lower sphere
by an auntie).

Since most people spend between six and ten hours there,
only a fraction of the time is given to sex proper. The rest
is devoted to the most unabashed voyeurism, from extremely
close range, upon pairs, trios, or more of performers, who
remain quite undisturbed by the audience. Any activity invol-

(20)

Point Lookout

Jitterbug at Point Lookout

ving anything the remotest bit unusual, or a fellatee of
noteworthy pulchritude or inchitude, brings a crowd of from
three to thirteen. A remark equally replete with fitness and
humor was addressed to one such audience by a queen upon
rising from her completed oral activity, "The next class will
be held at 4 P.M. on Tuesday."

     Most of the attendants are straight and occasionally one
puts in a rather silly appearance with a flashlight which may
or may not cause any change of activity. The piece de
resistance of any evening is the appearance of a
pulchritudinous sailor or soldier desiring a maximum of
blowjobs in a minimum period of time, and the consequent
rivalry for the honors, which may result in the formation of a
cartel at times. Of innocent arrivals there seem to be none.

     In an average 12 hours between 8 PM Saturday and 8 AM
Sunday, there are probably a spurt or two of a thousand

(21)

orgasms within the sacred confines, yielding somewhat over two quarts of digested and scattered come.

There are, of course, many other Turkish Baths in New York, the next most famous being the Times Square Baths. But neither the latter nor any of the others, no matter what their occasional activity, can boast of a reputation even approximating that of Everard's.

POOLS
There is no outstanding gay pool. For some time, the Shelton Hotel, already mentioned for its t-room, was considered the nearest thing, but it does not amount to much.

Some queens occasionally go to the St. George, just over in Brooklyn, which is probably the all-around best pool in Greater New York, but the gay proportion here is in general trivial. The number of beautiful straight youths, however, in this pool (and of course lockers and showers) is enormous.

(22)

Point Lookout

BEACHING

In the summer, one of New York's most delightful features
is Bitches' Beach (or, Queens' Beach) near Point Lookout,
L.I., which on Saturdays and Sundays is packed with hundreds
of faggots. Trains are taken from Penn Station to Long Beach,
and thence the Pt. Lookout bus. At a point referred to by the
bus-drivers as "Times Square", a privately-owned tract along
the water, all faggots (usually about 90% of the bus-load)
swish out of the bus and onto the beach.

Just what part of the beach is most popular varies—
sometimes it is near the water and other times half-way
between the water and the hinterland.

Much as this may vary, the above hinterland, called
inaptly "The Dunes" and more aptly "The Jungle", always draws
a considerable attendance. Amid winding and criss-crossing
paths, flanked by tall willows and shrubs, there taketh place
an ample amount of cruising, groping, and downright cock-

(23)

sucking, all in an atmosphere strongly resembling a Turkish Bath. But meanwhile, the patron gets browned too—by the sun, that is.

On some occasions, a gay vaudeville show is put on by some of the more talented of the patrons. This, however, tends to draw a considerable number of tourists as well as queens, and inevitably, someone doesn't like something and complains to the local police, with unfortunate results.

Some of the piss-elegant set patronize the beach at Fire Island, which is even harder to get to than Point Lookout. At the opposite extreme, some of the lowlier faggots on occasion form a large party to take over a section of Coney Island, New York's largest and commonest beach. Both of these, however, are distinctly insignificant compared to Bitches' Beach, which is by far the outstanding common meeting-ground for all classes of New York faggotry.

(24)

EATING PLACES

Like most cities, New York unfortunately has no universally popular gay rendezvous, either for meals or for after-hour snacks.

In the Village, the Jefferson Diner (6th Ave. & 8th St.) is the out-standing after-hours place, at its best at about 3 AM Sunday and often quite mad. The San Remo, on MacDougal St., draws some faggots now and then for both meals and snacks but remains substantially straight.

In the Midtown area, the Garden Cafeteria (8th Ave. & 50th) draws a certain number of faggots for both meals and after-hour snacks. Like-wise some of the Horn and Hardart Automats, most of all the one on 6th Ave. opposite Bryant Park. Despite clearly-manifested hostility by the management, the latter continues to draw the faithful patronage of the Bryant Parkites.

In this area, there are also

(25)

several French restaurants patronized by the more elegant: Larrés (56th St. east of 6th Ave.), Café Brittany (9th Ave. between 53rd and 54th) and the Du Midi (48th west of 8th Ave.). None of these, however, can be called gay.

Several of the bars are also patronized by the more elegant ones for meals too, such as the New Towne and the Sazarac. For the upper west side, the Stanwood Cafeteria (Bway south of 72nd) occasionally flourishes, especially near bar-closing time (for New Verdi patrons).

ROOMING

Certainly every red-blooded faggot visiting New York without previous residential arrangements will want to stop at another of S-on-H's outstanding attractions, the William Sloane Y (34th and 9th Ave.). It should not be necessary to mention such special centers of attraction as the showers, although some allusion might be made to the eastern T-room on the 3rd floor.

(26)

Away from the Crowd...

A word of caution must be included, however, as regards the staff. Hourly inspections are made on each floor after 9. The later it is, the more   likely an untoward creak or slurp will break through the nocturnal stillness.   This results in the door being opened immediately, and the victims told to   dress, pack, leave and never darken their door again (except under another name).   The NYPD, however, are not brought onto the scene. Obviously, activity between 5 and 9 is safer than after 9.

The other major Y, at 63rd and CPW, has a certain amount of activity in the basement T-room, but because of the restrictions on visitors (in marked contrast to the open-door policy at Sloane) and the more permanent set-up, has comparatively little activity on the upper floors and is not in the same class as Sloane House.

PRIVATE APARTMENTS
An enormous amount of activity,

(27)

40

...and into the Dunes.

especially parties and dances, naturally takes place in private apartments but this is both beyond the scope of this work, and hardly practicable to mention here.

BOOKS

Almost all works on ye subject, everything from The Scarlet Pansy to Kraff-Ebing, can be bought at one or all of the following three stores:

Midtown Book Shop—6th Ave. N of 42nd
Publishers Outlet—254 West 42nd St.
Times Sq. Book Shop—225 W. 42nd St.

A CLOSING NOTE

This booklet has been made as complete as possible at the time of publication, but each week or month brings changes. It is up to you to keep it up to date by making use of the ample space under "Memoranda and Addenda". For further information, call

RUddy 1-4692.

(28)

The
GAY GIRL'S GUIDE
(First Edition)
1949

The
GAY GIRL'S GUIDE

(First Edition)

A Primer for Novices
A Review for Roués

SWASARNT NERF
Co-Editor of Gaedeker's Sodom-on-Hudson

PETER ASTI
Cruising Editor of The Queen's Gazette

DAPHNE DILLDOCK
Professor of Clitorology, Gomorrah U.

A Phallus Press Publication
1949

The
GAY GIRL'S GUIDE
(First Edition)

A Primer for Novices
A Review for Roués

SWASARNT NERF
Co-Editor of Gaedeker's Sodom-on-Hudson

PETER ASTI
Cruising editor of The Queen's Gazette

DAPHNE DILLDOCK
Professor of Clitorology, Gomorrah U.

A Phallus Press Publication
1949

CONTENTS

Preface

Girl:

This booklet has been procured for you through the kindness of
your dear mother (or perhaps, sister).

It has been given to you to study in order that you might be as
fully prepared as possible to enjoy the full fruits. . .

Because of the survival of various archaic laws, it might be just
as well if you don't leave it lying around. An extra envelope,
with a sender's identification designed to dull almost anybody's
curiosity, has been provided. You can keep the booklet in this
envelope, or else you can use the envelope to mail it to someone
else.

Should you insist on giving a copy to someone of doubtful gaiety,
it might be advisable to first remove pages 48 to 58 with your
sewing scissors.

(2)

AUNTIE: Homosexual past 40, desperate,
              shameless and abject, generally
              pursues extreme youth.
BASKET: Male genitals as outlined against
              thin or tight clothing, generally
              used in connection with sailor
              pants, levis or swimming trunks.
BELLE: Used with various connotations,
              such as 1) any homosexual; 2) a
              young, flashy and possibly beau-
              tiful homosexual. Often used
              interchangeably with QUEEN.

B-J: Abbreviation for Blow-Job (See SWL)

*Terms are general American unless city
 or region is denoted; BCN stands for
 British Commonwealth of Nations. MBS stands
 for Male Bobby-Soxer. SWL is abbreviation
 for Supplementary Word List.

(3)

B-M: Abbreviation for "Bloody Mascu-
              line", BCN term synonymous with
              BUTCH.
BRING OUT: To introduce to the mysteries
              of homosexuality. See MOTHER
              and DAUGHTER.
BROWN: To have anal intercourse, with
              reference to active partner.
BROWNING-QUEEN: A homosexual whose
              principal sexual inte-
              rest is anal. Properly
              used with reference to
              passive partner, loose-
              ly used for active one
              too (for which, rarely,
              BROWNING-KING).
BUCKET: Posterior (clothed outline).
BUTCH: Not homosexual.
CAMP: As a verb, to display one's homo-
              sexual attributes merrily. As a
              noun, one who puts it on thickly.

(4)

e.g., "She's such a camp." Also
BCN adjective equivalent to GAY.

CAMPY: Very GAY, with humorous connota-
tion. Mostly a BCN term.

CHICKEN: Adolescent, homosexual or not.

CHOCOLATE: A Negro.

CLIP-QUEEN: A second cousin to DIRT and
usually a young, commercially-
inclined homosexual without
any desire for violence,
i.e. a sneak-thief.

COME OUT: To be initiated into the mysteries of homosexuality.

COMMERCIAL: One who is a male prostitute,
whether brazenly or discreetly,
homosexual or not. (adjective).

CRUISE: As a transitive verb, to seek
to catch the eye of someone in whom
one is interested, after

(5)

placing oneself in his vicinity,
or at least within his vision.
As an intransitive verb, to be
"on the make", to be looking
for someone of interest.

CRUISY: NYC MBS adjective for any kind
of place in which it's fun to
cruise or fool around.

CUNT: Mock-derogatory vocative used in
"bitchy" conversation.

DAISY-CHAIN: Homosexual activity, anal,
oral, or in combination,
involving more than two
persons.

DARLING: Meaningless vocative loosely
used in "bitchy" conversation
(Also in usual sense between
lovers, of course).

DAUGHTER: Male whom one has BROUGHT OUT.
Used also humorously in conversation or correspondence
in mock depreciation of one-

(6)

48

DIKE: self or the other party as a
             MOTHER.
DIKE: Lesbian, female homosexual.
DILL-DOCK: Artificial penis strapped on
             by active Lesbian partner.
DIRT: Properly, a highly specialized
             type of criminally psychopathic
             youth, self-appointed nemesis of
             any and all homosexuals, usually
             not homosexual himself (but this
             varies greatly since some kind of
             sexual abnormality or inferiority
             is almost always at the root of
             it), who guilefully leads on a
             homosexual interested in him until
             in a position to do him dirt, roll-
             ing and/or beating him up (rarely
             fatally), alone or with others,
             before or after being "blown". By
             extension, anyone following the
             above line of conduct, thus also
             including sailors, strong-armed
             CLIP-QUEENS, opportunistic ROUGH
             and COMMERICAL TRADE, et al.

(7)

DO: To fellate, blow, bring to an orgasm
               orally.
DO FOR TRADE: To DO without reciprocation
                   (See TRADE below).
DOLL: As a vocative, synonymous with
               DARLING. Also used in usual sense
               for a beautiful kid.
DRAG: Female attire.
DRAG-QUEEN: One who makes a living doing
               female impersonations in a
               DRAG-SHOW, or otherwise appears
               frequently in DRAG.
ELEGANT: Adjective used for homosexual
               who prides himself on his higher
               social level, as regards
               behavior, haunts, friends, con-
               versation, etc., in comparison
               with his more sordid brethren.
               The word has implications of
               both snobbishness and repression.

                        (8)

FISH: A woman (usually excluding Lesbians)
FISH-QUEEN: Properly, a "cunt-sucker", but in
               general usage applied to any
               homosexual who makes a point of
               bringing women with him where they'll
               be seen by his friends, with the
               apparent aim of of convincing
               himself and others he's bisexual.
FIX UP: Least gay euphemism for "Blow",
               used by some effeminophobic
               homosexuals. Rare.
FRENCH: Another, and quasi-straight,
               euphemism for "blow" or DO.
G.T.B.O.T.O.:   Boston MBS abbreviation
                   for "Get the basket on
                   that one."
GAY: Homosexual, queer (adj.). The only
               word used by homosexuals with ref-
               erence to themselves, their friends
               their haunts, etc.

                        (9)

50

GAY TRADE: Male who wants to be "blown"
but will not reciprocate. He
may be otherwise GAY himself,
or bisexual, and will kiss,
pet and perform other expected
requirements.

GET YOU!: Who do you think you're kidding!
("Get..." is used in an infinite
number of phrases).

GIRL: As a vocative, synonymous with
DARLING. Also used loosely by
homosexuals with reference to
themselves and their friends.

GLORY-HOLE: Phallic size hole in partition
between toilet booths. Some-
times used also for a mere
peep-hole.

GO DOWN ON: A quasi-straight term for
DO, "blow", etc.

GROPE: To feel someone's penis (usually

(10)

52

	with reference to semi-public con-ditions where one must remain more or less clothed.
GUM:	Boston MBS abbreviation for "Get-U-Mary!".
HEAD-QUEEN:	Homosexual whose chief operating areas are toilets.
HUNTER:	Passé term for homosexual who is constantly cruising and looking for new affairs, e.g., a homo-sexual "wolf".
JADE:	Connecticut synonym for AUNTIE.
JAM:	Adjective synonymous with BUTCH.
JOHN:	NYC term for an AUNTIE with finan-cial potentialities, on a long- or short-term basis (in contrast to which an AUNTIE becomes a poor JOHN).
KAI-KAI:	NYC MBS term. As an adjective, anally-minded. As a verb, to have sex with someone.

(11)

KANISH:	NYC MBS term for ass-hole, used with ref. to anal intercourse.
LILY:	MBS term for a policeman. Often, LILY LAW (especially in plural).
LUSH:	NYC MBS term for a terribly attractive but incorrigibly heterosexual young man.
M^2	BCN term for Mutual Masturbation.
MAD:	Extremely or excessively GAY. Loosely used with many shades of meaning.
MADAM BLUE:	New Jersey MBS name for a policeman.
MEAT:	Penis.

(12)

MOTHER: Male who has BROUGHT OUT subject.
             Also used humorously in conver-
             sation or correspondence (see
             DAUGHTER).
NINETY-SIX: California term for recipro-
             cal anal intercourse.
ONCER: Passé term for homosexual addicted
             to "one-night-stands".
PEASANT: Term of contempt used by the
             ELEGANT, or others jokingly
             affecting elegance, for those
             socially beneath them.
PERSONALITY: Northern New England euphe-
             mism for BASKET.
PISS-ELEGANT: Extremely ELEGANT.
QUEEN: Used with various connotations,
             like BELLE, such as 1) any homo-
             sexual; 2) a passé BELLE, 3) a
             very MAD BELLE. This popular
             and common word is found as a
             suffix (-Queen) in innumerable

(13)

54

REAM: compounds, to denote a homosexual specializing in any activity.

REAM: To insert one's tongue in partner's anal opening.

RIM: To lick one's partner's anal opening as the extreme expression of love, adoration or masochism.

ROUGH TRADE: Generally used in contrast to GAY TRADE as indicating subject will not even kiss, and is thus of untainted normality. Basically, a straight one who just likes to be "blown", though a completely homosexual person can assume this role on occasion too. Highly prized by many BELLES in reaction to their usual effeminate asso-ciates (often those who have re-ceived jeers or jibes from past partners because of their own inadequacies respecting size or coming-time convince themselves they don't really care about being

(14)

"blown" any more, and become TRADE-QUEENS). Sometimes used incorrectly as synonymous with DIRT, though there is no implication of violence in the term.

'ROUND THE WORLD: The kissing, sucking and licking of all parts of partner's body, front and rear, with heaviest emphasis on genital area.

SEA-FOOD: A Sailor, Coast Guardsman (or Sea Scout?), homosexual or not.

SEND UP: BCN verb for informing in a de-risive manner that one is not impressed by affectations or aloofness of the target. Remarks are usually made loudly or shouted at a distance, with much use of "Get..."

SISTER: A intimate friend and confidant who is not a lover.

(15)

SIXTY-NINE:	Properly, simultaneous oral intercourse, head to penis, but frequently used with reference to any kind of oral action, in contrast to anal.
SOIXANTE-NEUF:	French for SIXTY-NINE, used by the ELEGANT.
STRAIGHT:	Synonym for JAM, BUTCH, et al.
SWISH:	Used as a noun, verb and adjective (as adjective, usually SWISHY) with reference to extreme effeminacy in appearance and behavior.
TEA:	Marijuana.
TEAROOM (T-ROOM):	Men's room, toilet.
TOURIST:	Term of contempt used by habitués of a certain place for an unfamiliar and curious-looking intruder, whether straight or homosexual.
TRADE:	General term for one who wants to

(16)

be "blown" without reciprocating, and with no commercial implication per se. Divides into subordinate classes, such as GAY TRADE, ROUGH TRADE, COMMERCIAL TRADE, and possibly also DIRT.

TRADE-QUEEN:	One who prefers merely to "DO FOR TRADE".
TRICK:	Chicago term for someone on whom subject has designs, is trying to make, etc.
UPSET:	Verb used with various connotations. As a transitive verb, to disturb someone's equilibrium, from the point of view of
	1) lost dignity, composure, aloofness, peace of mind, etc.
	2) erotic stimulation (with an erection generally understood).
	As an intransitive verb, usually used with the erotic and erectile implication, e.g., "he gets me all upset."

(17)

Supplementary Word List

The following words or phrases are
frequently used, seriously or
facetiously, in a sense the same
as, or equivalent to, their meaning in straight English (slang).

AFFAIR	DOLL	LOVER
BITCH(Y)	FABULOUS	MAKE
BLOW	FAGGOT	MARRIED
BLOW-JOB	FAIRY	NECK
BOX	FRENCH-KISS	NORMAL
COCK	FUCK	ONE-NIGHT-STAND
COCK-SUCKER	HARD-ON	QUEER (FOR)
COME (n. & v.)	HUSBAND	SLUT
CUTE	KEPT	SUCK
DADDY	KISS	WHORE

(18)

TECHNIQUES

There are three main groups of techniques. They are the
oral, the anal and the miscellaneous which we will arbitrarily
call mutual masturbatory. In the various possible combinations,
quite a large number of relationships can be evolved from these
basic groups.

To some extent, it is possible to predict to which
technique a certain person is partial by his general
characteristics and behavior but such predictions are notoriously
subject to exceptions.

For instance, generally speaking, the orally-minded are the
most concerned with the factors of youth, looks and genital
dimensions. Conversely, the ones who show no great interest in
the genital dimensions, age or looks of their potential partners
are very likely to be anally-minded (assuming they are not
commercial).

(19)

In general, cocksucking talent is directly proportional to age. The very young have usually neither desire nor talent, and if they have desire, their talent is very mediocre. Talent and desire seem to both increase with age, and whether it is due to psychological or physiological reasons, there are very few really top-notch cocksuckers far short of forty.

It is also worth nothing that among youthful cocksuckers, talent is in inverse proportion to swishiness. Almost always, the more obvious, the less talent; the least obvious, the most talented.

ORAL

This is the technique which has become most generally associated with homosexuality (at least where bathing facilities are available on a mass basis), though it may be that only about half of all homosexual affairs center around it.

The idyllic form is "sixty-nine" in which each partner places his head

(20)

ORAL

more or less in line with the other's penis, which he proceeds to suck. Under ideal but rare conditions, the two will come at the same time. There are slight variations of the position. Thus, each may be more or less reposing on his side, or one may actually be on top of the other partner.

The chief advantage of "sixty-nine" is the psychological one. Neither partner can be involved in a superiority-inferiority relationship implied when one has "gone down on" the other. Furthermore there can remain no anxiety as to whether after one partner has been brought to an orgasm, he may proclaim himself unable to reciprocate.

On the other hand, "sixty-nine" has distinct disadvantages over other oral forms. Firstly, the position decreases each person's oral manoeuverability. Secondly, the distraction at one end is likely to slow down, or for moments even sidetrack, his abilities at the other end. Thirdly, the tongue, which can

(21)

play an important part in the fine art of cocksucking, is of necessity on the upper side of the penis, where it is less likely to prove as satisfying as on the lower side, and with some people may even prove downright unpleasant.

Perhaps less idyllic, but of far greater efficacy, are the rotational forms, which are sometimes included under "69" when the latter is used with reference to any oral form. In this case, each partner "does" the other in turn. Usually the more experienced one will be "done" first, since he is by long practice better equipped to face the ordeal of "doing" his partner after he himself has come. If the partners have had previous affairs, they will know of any great difference in each other's timing, in which case obviously the one who comes easier should be "done" last.

Common sense should dictate that where "69" proper does not produce simultaneous orgasms, the partner who has not

(22)

come should be given the benefits inherent in the other form. Yet many, for a combination of reasons centering around pride and esthetics, will refuse to engage in any oral activity unless they are in the "69" position.

There are two primary factors that determine the good cocksucker. They may be summed up as DEPTH and SPEED.

"Depth" refers to the necessity of taking at least half of the length of the erect penis, and preferably more. "Speed" refers to the necessity of matching, orally, the rhythm and tempo which naturally precedes an orgasm, whether in heterosexual, anal, oral or masturbatory activity (slightly over one per second).

The novice tends to violate both these important rules, by taking only the head of the penis into his mouth, and moving his mouth very slowly, which is often partially explained by his initial repulsion. These two points are most important of all at the time of or-

(23)

gasm, and it is at just this time that the novice tends, because of his anxiety about the disposition of the ensuing flow of semen, to slow down his movements and have the minimum phallic content in his mouth. The result is invariably highly unsatisfactory to his partner.

Two secondary factors that also play their part are worth a brief note. The ability to produce a great deal of saliva at the time is obviously most helpful (The amount of saliva will generally be in direct proportion to the sex appeal of the one being "done", there being a substantial amount of truth in the expression "drool over"). And of equally obvious benefit is a fairly large mouth.

If he has a sufficiently large mouth, and has mastered the factors of speed, depth and saliva, the novice has become a good cocksucker. Only a great natural aptitude will enable him to pass beyond this rating to attain a truly superb status.

(24)

It should be noted that there are also several positions in which it is the partner who is being "done" who does everything, as in intersexual activity, with the other partner merely keeping his mouth wide open (but using his tongue suitably). The one who is "being done" thus controls his own speed—and to some extent, depth—which makes it a preferable form to many, and it is equally preferable to some cocksuckers. Both partners may be lying on their sides, with the one who is "being done" higher up on the bed, or the latter may be kneeling over his prone partner's head.

In addition to the above oral activity proper, supplementary actions are in order when an affair takes an oral turn, and these the novice will master with time and practice. On the way "down" (primarily with the rotational type), it is customary to kiss, lick and suck various additional parts of the partner's body, such as the neck, nipples, navel and testicles. If done

(25)

really extensively, to the entire back and front, and especially in the nether region, the term "around the world" is applied. Lapping of the ear-drums is also very easy and very effective, and should very early become part of the novice's repertoire.

In some cases, with the apparent motivation of either masochism or extreme adoration, we find the extremes of "rimming", where the tongue is moved around the anal opening, and "reaming", where the tongue is inserted inside the anal opening.

These subordinate practices will naturally vary greatly between different sets of partners, and the extreme sado-masochistic inventions will rarely be of concern to the novice. These practices can come into play with techniques other than the oral, but it is most generally then that they do occur.

There is sometimes an issue over

(26)

whether to swallow or eject the semen. Sometimes the most ardent of cocksuckers profess an inability to swallow it and the necessity to eject it. This must be viewed on a psychological basis (they feel that they oughtn't to enjoy it so much and ought to feel some disgust somewhere along the line), for where there is genuine repulsion, it must be because of the taste. Yet the taste remains longer when the semen is retained for those few additional seconds before a decent manner of ejecting it can be resorted to; when swallowed at once, the taste remains for a much shorter period. By this defense mechanism, they give due compensation to the disgust they feel they should have, and don't.

The taste will, of course, vary surprisingly from person to person, sometimes very mild, sometimes very tangy. But in each and every case, the faster it is swallowed, the less time the taste remains. It is doubtful that there is any genuine allergy to semen.

(27)

ANAL

On the whole, there is much less range of variation and subject for comment in anal activity.

Only in the question of positions is there any real variation. The most common is probably that in which both partners are on their sides. Next most common is perhaps that in which the passive partner is lying on his stomach, with the active partner on top of him.

Most all-around satisfying is the position most difficult for the passive partner to master. A pillow is placed under his posterior, and his legs are then drawn up towards his chin, with more enjoyable face-to-face intercourse in the traditional intersexual position, and with kissing highly feasible. A slight variation of this position has the passive partner throw one leg over the active partner's shoulder.

Least romantic, but most easy for the passive novice to master, is the position in which he sits down on the

(28)

erect penis of the not-so-active active partner he is facing.

"Browning", as it is termed, should not be tried in the absence of a lubricant. Most popular is K-Y. Vaseline will do almost equally well. The elegant have been known to favor Wildroot Cream Oil or various kinds of cold creams. In emergencies, saliva is sometimes made to help.

There is little need for instruction to the active partner, since he is not called upon to do anything an animal can't do. For the passive partner, to be able to "take it", the prime prerequisite is the ability to relax at will, which takes a certain amount of muscular coordination. The really adept have the same preference for the largest of penes, claiming that the largest inserted carefully can cause less pain or discomfort that the smallest inserted hurriedly or without care. The less adept may be partial to small and thin ones.

(29)

ANAL

It is obvious how the active partner comes, but there is much room for variation in determining how the inactive partner comes. He may turn active himself, if his partner is also adept at the passive role. His partner may "do"   him, or may simply finish the job manually (the most professedly normal of active partners may refuse to perform even this function and leave it to their passive partner). Or the passive partner may resort to one of the abdominal variants to be mentioned below.

While there is a sentimental value in simultaneous orgasms, there is no physiological point to it, since the passive partner can rarely feel the active partner's orgasm.

The passive partner's excellence is obviously to be measured primarily in terms of the phallic quantity he can take, the ease with which he can take it, and in the case of the really adept, the amount of additional suction power he manages to provide.

(30)

ANAL

The active partner's excellence has to be measured in terms of his care, his gentleness (except to the masochist), perhaps the subtlety with which he intro- duces the lubricant, and most of all in connection with how he simultaneously or afterwards (rarely previously) satisfies his partner. As in all cases, the kissing and general love-play is of obvious importance.

ORAL-ANAL

This is a rare and idyllic combination, but one very difficult to master since it requires a great amount of contortionist prowess on the part of both partners (for which young and supple bodies are essential). One of them manages at the same time to "brown" and "blow" the other one. The position is a variation of the one covered in para. 3 of the anal discussion above. The oral end of it can never be very satisfying since little "depth" is possible.

(31)

MUTUAL MASTURBATORY (MISCELLANEOUS).

There are quite a few different variations under this general, and somewhat arbitrary, heading. The most simple consists of each partner bringing the other to an orgasm solely by his hand.

A more complicated, and more popular, form makes use of the usual heterosexual position, with one partner on top of, and facing, the other, so that the penis of each one is in motion against the close-pressed abdomen of the other. In general, this method is employed only where both partners are circumcised (or the one using it when the other partner has already come), since it causes excessive strain on the more delicate uncircumcised penes.

Other variations make use of the same principle—against the thighs, between the legs, and the oft-joked about "under the arm".

(32)

These techniques have one great advantage: they enable both partners to be kissing rapturously at the moment of orgasm.

CONCLUSION

In general, where an affair lasts through repeated occasions, the technique is likely to be other than oral.

A fair estimate might be that of pairs that have been going steadily and faithfully for more than a month, 50% employ a mutual masturbatory variant, 40% a "browning" combination and only 10% oral. (In the sum total of all affairs in the American homosexual world, however brief, over a given period such as a year, the percentage of cases in which at least one partner is "blown" is probably as high as around 70%).

The reasons are not too hard to find. For most people, a lingering self-consciousness about the oral, however slight, tends to disassociate it

(33)

from love of a persons esteemed in a sense beyond the physical.

On the other hand, those who gain nothing but sheer pleasure from the oral are likely to lean towards an unending variety of experience, and therefore disdain wasting too much time on any one person.

Finally, all long-range affairs are likely to be founded on the most rapturous and harmonious of kissing, and a natural tendency to want to be engaged in it as the moment of orgasm. While kissing is almost always present with the mutual masturbatory combinations, and may be present with the anal, it obviously cannot be present with the oral.

KISSING

This technique not being a homosexual one (exclusively), a discussion of it does not properly belong here.

(34)

KISSING

Nevertheless, it should be noted that kissing of the type described as "French-kissing" or "soul-kissing" plays a very deep part in all but the most fleeting affairs, and might be considered as the common denominator amidst all other variations. Whether or not an individual will "French-kiss" with real ardor with a member of his own sex is probably the best single determinant as to whether he can be considered "gay".

Because of the ease with which it can be mastered, the novice should become expert at it very soon. Excellence is simply a result of will: he who tries passionately and moves his tongue actively against his partner's, and tries hard to emulate all his partner's tricks, will soon be as proficient as the best.

(35)

How to Distinguish Readily Between the
Gay and Various Types of Trade

While there are no fool-proof ways for determining in advance the facts about someone in whom you are interested, there are certain things to look for that will stand up in the great majority of cases. We will start with the least gay and work our way up to the most completely gay.

DIRT vs. ROUGH TRADE

Rough trade will be found to maintain a passive attitude replete with remnants of pride, self-respect and early sexual conditioning. He will rarely do anything until you start talking to him, and will wait for you to make all leading suggestions.

Dirt, on the other hand, has no such compunctions. He has a positive and primary object: to beat up and/or roll queers. He will not hesitate to make the first

(36)

move, to open the conversation, etc. and in no time will be suggesting going for a walk or going over to your place (rarely to his). He never has a sense of humor or a natural smile.

From the point of view of social background, the real dirt type almost always comes from that class that produces most psychopathic types, the petty bourgeoisie, and rarely, as the less informed might believe, from the proletariat. Rough trade may come from any class.

The above refers mostly to outdoor places, such as parks and streets. Dirt rarely operates out of bars. The same is true of movie theaters, where the activities, whether in seats or pissoirs, are incompatible with dirt psychology, e.g. an active approach, with only words as bait, and nothing physical to compromise his belligerently normal self-convictions (or to expose his sexual inadequacies).

(37)

74

Beware of well-built, well-dressed, good-looking youths who, while they don't sound gay, are ready to take the initiative at every turn, and may drop hints and phrases, without humor, to suggest that they have been around!!!!

ROUGH TRADE vs. GAY TRADE

Here we are confronted with something of a conflict over definition.

"Gay Trade" can really refer either to someone who makes no bones about being queer, but is simply against cock-sucking, or to someone who considers himself basically straight, but enjoys a little kissing before he gets "blown", and is not squeamish about his kissing partner's sex.

In any event, kissing is obviously the key factor, so the quickest and simplest way of deciding which category the person in question falls into is to get some place where kissing is feasible, however briefly. If he refuses,

(38)

76

to kiss at all, or will not French-kiss, he will almost always fall into the rough trade category, and it is up to your own personal preferences whether you still remain interested (we must say "almost always" because there is also a category, usually of proletarian origin, for which there is no name, which is quite adept at cock-sucking, but loathes kissing).

It might seem that this test is silly, since the test is merely the same as the definition. However, the kissing is the primary factor, the answer here will also determine other variable conditions of your relationship with the person in question.

GAY TRADE vs. GAY

There is a very simple little test that is reasonably accurate. Under amorous circumstances where there is a certain amount of darkness and privacy, such as in movie seats, on a couch or in a dark outdoor place, and

(39)

erections are produced, it is important whether he gropes you or not after you have groped him, in more than a token fashion. Gay trade will rarely grope with any real enthusiasm. (It might also be noted, along lines of this test, that rough trade will rarely even get an erection without direct manual stimulation; and, to neatly carry the point further, dirt will often fail to get an erection even with manual stimulation, relative impotence being frequently a factor in the psychopathic condition of dirt.

SUMMARY

The above tests apply best under the purest conditions, e.g. in parks and movies. In bars, things can be more confused. In really gay bars there will rarely be any dirt. On the other hand, a thorough-going faggot can play rough trade for commercial purposes. This type can be distinguished by an apparent preference for, or at least lack of object-

(40)

ions to, the attentions of conspicuously old, or repulsive admirers. Occasionally, the anal-passive type exhibits this same behavior, without any commercial implications, and by genuine preference.

In bars, where the emphasis is on talk rather than action, it is mostly through your eyes and ears, over a longer period of time (than in the simple outdoor tests) that you will have to decide whether he's gay, gay trade, or rough trade.

(41)

GAY LIFE IN THE U.S.A.

Conditions prevailing in the U.S. represent a compromise between two opposing forces. On the one hand, we have a maximum of personal and social liberty and freedom of movement available to all individuals and groups in the U.S. as nowhere else in the world. On the other hand, we have a very definite legal repression of homosexuality as severe in Anglo-Saxon law as in any legal system derived from Judaeo-Christian taboos.

The only significant agent of repression is, of course, the local police. However, in the absence of   strong pressures upon them from civic or religious groups, few local police departments will cause much difficulty. One important reason is that the same Anglo-Saxon law which outlaws homosexuality also requires precise proofs of its occurrence, which proof the police can rarely secure without taking the risk of violating laws or customs in the process.

(42)

In the case of bars, it is customary in any metropolis for the proprietor to pay "protection" money to the local police department to further guarantee their indifference.

There are, however, two cases where the police will often take action. The first regards minors. Conditioned by sentimental Irish drivel about the purity and innocence of children, the police seem to feel that while adults are incorrigible and hopeless, minors may be "corrected" and saved. Anyone thus subject to suspicion of intercourse with, or designs upon, a minor is much more likely to have trouble with the police than if subject to similar suspicions in connection with an adult. While something may be said for this attitude when it protects really ambivalent straight minors, it is a farce when applied to little, juvenile whores.

(43)

GAY LIFE IN THE U.S.A.

The second case is where the police are subject to strong pressure from civic or religious groups of one sort or another, which pressure is usually the result of indiscreet local excesses. Thereupon the police usually make some raids upon parks and bars a few times over a period of a few weeks, and then the whole thing is forgotten again for an indefinite period.

Occasionally, however, the pressure is so great that the effect tends to be far more disastrous and semi- permanent, as with the Great Purges—Madison in 1945, Los Angeles in 1946, and Chicago in 1949.

The centers in the U.S. are, obviously enough, in the major cities, and for the most part, the degree of activity is in direct proportion to the size of the city. These major cities can be divided into two main categories: 1) the permanent, native-population type; and 2) the transient or tourist type.

(44)

The tourist type of city is limited to a smaller number, but these seem to be of greater attraction. First and foremost is New York, followed by Los Angeles (as it recovers from the purge of '47), Miami, New Orleans and to some extent, San Francisco.

First and foremost of the native population category, until the great purge of '49, was Chicago, followed by San Francisco (sort of half and half), Philadelphia, Boston, Washington, St. Louis, Indianapolis, Detroit and Baltimore. Less important are Seattle, Dallas and a host of others which nevertheless have their faithful devotees.

One cannot say arbitrarily which type is the best. The tourist-type cities offer: greater variety of dis- traction, human and material. The permanent-type cities usually offer a finer human variety, and are especially superior for "chicken". People are more sincere and friendly here, turn-

(45)

ing to the gaudy and artificial (and among the younger, to the commercial) in the tourist-type cities. Yet one   is more likely to get bored sooner in the permanent-type, so that it remains essentially a matter of your personal taste and preference.

From a general geographic point of view, the cities in the northern half of the country are more all-   around attractive than those in the southern half. For all the attractions of their weather and color, Los Angeles, New Orleans, Miami et al. cannot measure up to New York, Chicago (pre-Purge), San Francisco, et al., all things considered.

In coming to an end of this discussion of American Gay Life, it seems worth noting that in no other country   in the world is the homosexual population less subversive and a more ardent supporter of the prevailing culture. Without doubt this is due to the fact

(46)

that American culture is a female culture, in which the norms are determined by female sentiments rather than male sentiments. The worship of youth, beauty and fine clothing, the gaudy advertising, the cult of the theatrical world of Broadway and Hollywood, the juke boxes, are but a few examples.

In the following sections, you will find listed for your convenience a large number of "nerve centers" in different categories, of the Gay U.S.

It is inevitable that some of the places cited may no longer exist, or may no longer be "nerve centers" when and if you visit them. Such a list must needs be subject to constant revision.

In most cases, however, if you find only one place, of any category, still thriving in a given city, contacts made in this one place will soon provide the additional list desired.

(47)

WHERE TO MAKE CONTACTS

PARKS

The park forms the basic gay rendezvous in every city. It can be found merely by logical deduction, and through contacts made there, can provide the key to other phases of gay life in the town. Parks are permanent and unchanging from year to year. They cannot be permanently affected by raids.

Far from being in some out of the way corner of a town, the gay park is usually a smallish one in the downtown area, or in the center of the town. It may be called a "Square" and may not actually be a full-fledged park.

There will usually be one particular side, area or lane that is the real center of activity in the park. It is generally neither the most conspicuous nor the most obscure part, but rather, between these two extremes. For your convenience, here is a list of parks in some of the major cities:

(48)

PARKS

Boston: Botanical Gardens, side par-
                allel to Beacon Street.
Chicago: Grant Park, west side between
                    Randolph & Monroe Streets.
                Lincoln Park betw. Oak & Div-
                    ision Streets.
Los Angeles: Pershing Sq., eastern arm.
Miami: Bayfront Park, southern half.
                New York: Bryant Park, eastern side
                Central Pk. west of 62nd & 5th
                    "   "   east of 78th & CPW
                Riverside Pk, btw. 72 & 79 St
                Rockefeller Center, west side
New Orleans: Jackson Square
Philadelphia: Rittenhouse Square
San Francisco: Union Square
Washington: Lafayette Park

(49)

MOVIES

Although less basic than parks, since they are subject to change, the right movie house can be deduced logically, like the right park. But a particularly hostile management, imposing continual and careful supervision by a large staff, or by changing physical structure (especially in the case of T-rooms) can nullify any logic.

The gay movie will be one that does not have first-run features, yet presents a fairly attractive appear- ance inside and out. It will generally show pairs of new features just off the first-run, or revivals, or in rare cases, westerns or all-comic shows. It will be located in the downtown area or near the heart of town.

There are, of course, also some gay first-run theaters or neighborhood playhouses, but they are the exception.

A few noteworthy movie theaters in some key American cities:

(50)

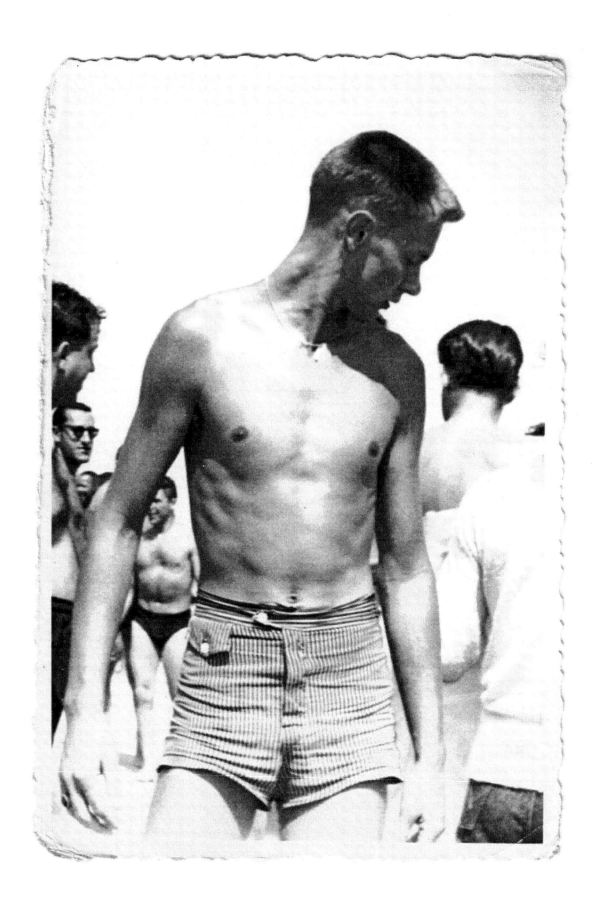

MOVIES

Boston: Victory; Orpheum

Chicago: McVickers; Oriental

New York
  Times Sq. Area (Almost all on 42nd
    between 6th & 8th Aves. Especially
    the Pix.)
  Lower East Side: Metropolitan (14th)
                    Lowe's Ave. B (5th)
                    Orpheum (8th St.)

New Orleans: Lyceum; Strand

Philadelphia: Family

San Francisco: Portola; State

(51)

BARS

    Bars are decidedly subject to change from year to year, and
often every few months. Furthermore, there is no way of
logically deducing which bars will be "gay bars". You simply
have to know before you go to the city, or else meet someone
there who can tell you the score.

    One little trick often works, if you can bring yourself to
do it: Get in a taxi and ask the driver to take you to "the
gayest bar in town". Whether it works depends on both the
knowledge and understanding of the cabbie.

    Most gay bars, like parks and movies, tend to be not too
far from the center of town. Most large cities have more than
one gay bar, and each one tends to cater to a different type, or
at least to be taken over by such types.

    In the following list, many will doubtless be passé by the
time you read this, or visit them, but that is inevitable.

(52)

Baltimore: Silver Dollar

Boston: Chess Room (Touraine), Phil
          Harris', Playland, Silver
          Dollar, Mardi Gras, Pot-o'Gold

Chicago: (Which of the "Near North" bars
          closed by the Purge will re-open
          again is anybody's guess.)

  Near North: Carousel, Glass Pub, White
                Spider, Windup (Benny the
                Bum's and Twelve O'Clock
                under unfriendly new man-
                agement before the Purge.)

  Division Street: No. 7, Innuendo, John's
  Loop: The Lome (Sherman)

Greater Los Angeles
  Downtown L.A.: Maxwell's, Tip-Top
  Hollywood-Beverly Hills: Bradley's
                            Black Watch
                            Gala

  Santa Monica: Hap's
Miami: Delicate Frank's, Jewel Box
Milwaukee: Legion, Royal Hotel

(53)

New York:
  Times Sq: Silver Rail, Ross' Backstage,
           Astor (passé)
  Upper West Side: New Verdi Square
  Middle East Side: Allan's, Blue Parrot,
              Golden Pheasant, Swan,
              Town Bar
  Village: MacDougal's, Mary's, Main St.
New Orleans:
  French Quarter: Tony Barcino's
              Lafitte's Garage Bar
              Starlet
  Modern Quarter: Dixie's Bar of Music
Norfolk: Lynd Haven
Philadelphia: Green Dragon, Maxine's
San Francisco: Jim Dolan's, Echo, 356
           Club, Black Cat
Washington: Casablanca, Chicken Hut,
        Deauville, Maystat

(54)

BARS

The above bars have been confirmed as still flourishing in
1948 or 1949. Some additional bars, less recently
confirmed:

Albany: Skippy's
Cincinnati: Cat & the Fiddle, Keyhole
Cleveland: Verdon Club, Musical Bar
Columbus, O.: Neal House
Dallas: Reno, Gypsy
Hartford: Adajian's Room, Bond Hotel,
        Red Stag, Ryan's Bar
Huntington: Martin's Grill, Monarch
         Café, Old Times Inc.
Little Rock: Brass Rail
Memphis: Creel Room (Peabody)
Minneapolis: Viking Room (Radison)
Oklahoma City: Bishop's

(55)

Rochester: Seneca Hotel
St. Louis: Chase Bar, Mme. Tooey's
St. Paul: Kitty Kurmser's
Salt Lake City: Overseas Club, Embassy
San Diego: Green Parrot
Santa Fé: La Fonda Hotel
Seattle: Snake Pit

(56)

BARS

This Guide is primarily for the U.S.A., but at this point
it might be worth noting a few gay bars in other countries
(NOT recently confirmed).

Canada
  Montreal: Dominion Square, Hawaiian
              Lounge, Penguin, Piel Tavern,
              Samovar, Tic-Toc
  Toronto: Beverage Room, Ford, Savarin
Mexico, Mexico City: Ritz Bar
Hawaii, Honolulu: Tropics, Wagon Wheel,
                   Waikiki Tavern
Eire, Dublin: Davy's, Dawson's
France, Paris: Boeuf-sur-le-toit
Great Britain:
  London: White Room
           Chelsea: George & the Dragon
                     Queen's Head
  Bristol: White Elephant

(57)

BEACHES AND BATHS

Although emphasis is placed on the maximum exposure of the male body in both these categories, there are distinct differences. Beaches have mostly youngish elements, baths a large number of "aunties". Beaches are free, baths quite expensive. Action on beaches is fairly unrestrained. Beaches are inevitably quite a ways from town (with the notable exception of Chicago's), baths usually near the center of town. A list of a few of each follows:

BEACHES
  Chicago: Oak Street Beach
  Greater L.A.: Santa Monica, w. of Hap's
  Miami: 23rd St. Beach, Miami Beach
  New York: Long Beach s. of Pt. Lookout
            Fire Island, northern tip

BATHS
  Chicago: Lincoln Baths
  New York: Everard Baths
  San Francisco: Jack's Baths
  Mexico City: St. Augustine Baths

(58)

1. FICTION

   A. Directly on Homosexuality

   Helen Anderson, Pity for Women. 1937.
      About dikes, of course.

   Dorothy Baker, Trio, 1943.
      A young college girl, her domi-
      neering old dike of a roommate
      And the boy friend, who wins.

   André Birabeau, Revelation. 1930.
      A French story. Momma's beloved
      boy is killed in an accident.
      She goes over his effects and
      finds letters from his lover,
      whom she thereupon determines
      to kill.

   John Horne Burns, The Gallery (Fifth
   Portrait, Momma). 1947.
      A splendid story about a gay
      bar in war time Italy, with
      superb dialogue and portraits.

(59)

LITERATURE—Fiction

Stuart Engstrand, The Sling and The
                    Arrow. 1947.
      A middle-aged businessman gets
      queerer and queerer, sends his
      wife off to the office, gets
      all upset by a sailor and ends
      up being chased around town in
      drag by the police.

Richard Erickson, Confessional
              "Cross-Section, 1947"
      A short story in which mother
      starts dropping nasty hints
      to sonny about his hero, a bach-
      elor friend of the family, who
      is finally confronted with the
      $64 question by sonny.

Diana Frederics, Diana. 1948.
      A dike's story.

Radclyffe Hall, The Well of Loneli-
                    ness, 1926.
      The classic Lesbian story, pio-
      neer of English fiction on
      homosexuality. Dull in spots.

(60)

LITERATURE—Fiction

Charles R. Jackson, <u>The Fall of Valor</u>. 1947.
    College professor and wife, their marital
    relations slipping, go off on a vacation
    together and become chummy with another
    couple. Prof. falls in love with the
    other husband and thinks he is getting
    somewhere until bashed on head.
Harlan McIntosh, <u>This Finer Shadow</u>. 1941.
    All wrapped up in complex Freudian
    overtones, it seems to be
    about a bisexual hero over whom
    faggots and fish struggle in
    vain. Very dull except for
    brilliant chapter XVI, the best
    ever written on a drag party,
    with marvelous dialog and description.
Thomas Mann, <u>Death in Venice</u>, 1925.
    While this may be tops in lite-
    rary value, it is a rather dull
    story about an old man drooling
    over a little Polish bitch (m.)

(61)

Mrs. Blair Niles, <u>Strange Brother</u>.
      1931, reprint 1949.
    A mediocre attempt at a counterpart to
    <u>The Well of Loneliness</u>, with a sensitive
    hero in his 20 who loves straight men
    but not faggots, and doesn't know what
    to do. Completely lacking in
    true color and dialog, but other-
    wise well written and readable.
Janet Schane, <u>The Dazzling Crystal</u>, '46.
    A woman, her husband, and his
    domineering old lover. The
    woman wins, of course.
Robert Scully, <u>The Scarlet Pansy</u>, n.d.
    Undated, and of mysterious origin,
    this delightful classic is <u>must</u> reading.
    Fay Etrange (Fr. for "queer fairy")
    referred to as "she" throughout the book, is a
    sort of faggotic Horatio Alger hero(ine),
    achieving success upon success in America
    and Europe between 1903 and 1918. Filled to

(62)

the brim with top-notch gay dia-
logue, double-entendres and color.
it has a sort of Dickens touch in style.
Andre Tellier, Twilight Men. 1931.
Tellier's attempt is better
than Niles's, but nowhere near
as good as Vidal or "Scully". The hero
is the young son of a French nobleman,
who despises him. He comes to New York and
becomes a success as a poet and
belle, and is even kept by a judge.
When his father's path crosses
his again, the inevitable tragedy
results.
Gore Vidal, The City and the Pillar. 1948.
A superb piece of work, the
best to date and unlikely to be surpassed.
Set in the U.S. between 1938 and 1946,
it concerns a handsome, six-foot Virginia blond who starts by fall-

(63)

ing in love with a straight chum, and thereafter
can't return anyone else's love, be it that of
movie idol or literary lion, or even of an exotic
and understanding fish. As his experience increases, he finds he's not so different from
the rest as he first thought, and thrives on
the hope that his true love has developed the
same way. When this hope proves vain, the inevitable tragic ending results. Splendidly written,
full of accurate dialog and color.

Anna Elisabet Weirauch, The Scorpion, '32.
                               The Outcast, '33.
About Lesbians.   Translated from
The German by Whittaker Chambers.

Gale Wilhelm, We Too Are Drifting, '35.
                  Torchlight to Valhalla, '37.
More about Lesbians.

(64)

B.   Indirectly or Partially on Hs.

(This category is huge, and could
begin with Plato's Republic and
Banquet. The following are merely
a partial and somewhat arbitrarily-
chosen handful. Space has been
left below for you to add any
recommendations you may receive
from other sources.)

Truman Capote, Other Voices, Other
          Rooms. 1948.
André Gide, The Counterfeiters (1928)
          The Immoralist (1936)
Marcel Proust, Cities of the Plain
     It is difficult to list this
     properly. The above title is the
     English title given to a translation of
     those books of the many-volume "Remem-
     brance of Things Past" with the most
     references to the subject. The
     French date is 1921-2, U.S. 1930.
Calder Willingham, End as a Man. 1946.

(65)

2.   Scientific and Non-Fiction
          The following can, of course,
          only be a partial selection.
          A very complete list will be
          found in Kinsey, pp. 766-787.
     G. Allen, The Sexual Perversions
          Abnormalities. London. 1940.
     American Journal of Orthopsychiatry.
          J.O. Wortis, Intersexuality and
               Effeminacy in the Male Homo-
               sexual. Volume X. 1940.
          A.N. Foxe, Psychoanalysis of a
               Sodomist. Vol. XI, 1941, 133-42.
          Bender, Lauretta & Paster, Homo-
               sexual Trends in Children.
               Volume XI, 1941, pp. 730-743.
     American Journal of Psychiatry.
          A.A. Brill, Homoeroticism and
               Paranoia, Vol. 13, 1934, 957-74.
          G.W. Henry & H.W. Galbraith,
               Constitutional Factors in Homo-
               sexuality. Vol. 13, 1934,
               pp. 1249-1270.

(66)

LITERATURE—Scientific

(Anonymous), The Invert and his Social
Adjustment. Baltimore, 1929.
Havelock Ellis, Studies in the Psycho-
logy of Sex (Vol 2, "Sexual Inver-
sion". Philadelphia, 1915).
Sigmund Freud, Three Contributions to
The Theory of Sex. (Reprint 1938).
Geoffrey Gorer, The American People.
NYC, 1948. Pages 125-130.
G. W. Henry, Sex Variants: A Study of
Homosexual Patterns. NYC, 1941.
Journal of Nervous and Mental Diseases.
M. Prince, Sexual Perversion or Vice?
A Pathological & Therapeutic Inqui-
ry. Volume 25, p. 237.
S.G. Williams, Homosexuality: a Bio-
logical Anomaly. Vol. 99, 1944.
Journal of Personality
T.V. Moore, Pathogenesis & Treatment
of Homosexual Disorders. XIV, 47-83.

(67)

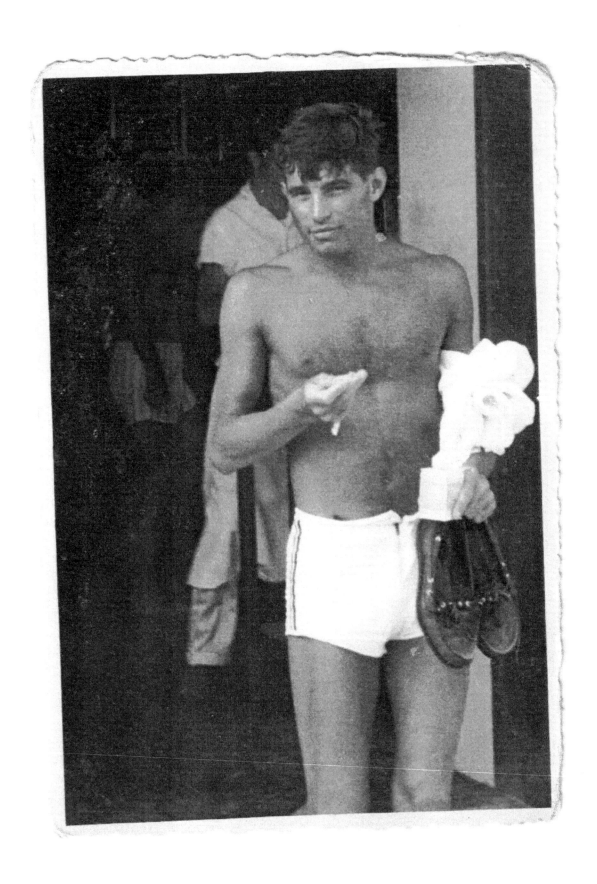

LITERATURE—Scientific

Kinsey, Pomeroy and Martin, Sexual Beha-
    vior in the Human Male. Ch. 21.
    Philadelphia, 1948.
Richard von Krafft-Ebing, Psychopathia
    Sexualis, Chs. 4-6. Leipzig, 1876.
Gregorio Maranon, The Evolution of Sex
    and Intersexual Conditions. Ch. 13.
    London, 1932.
Mental Hygiene.
    G. W. Henry & A.A. Gross, Social Fac-
    tors in the Case Histories of One
    Hundred Homosexuals. Vol. 22, 1938.
    G. W. Henry & A.A. Gross, The Homo-
    sexual Delinquent. Vol. 25, 1941.
Newsweek. Homosexuals in Uniform.
    June 9, 1947, p. 54.
Psychoanalytic Review.
    P. Schilder, On Homosexuality. XVI, '29
Wilhelm Stekel, Bisexual Love, Boston,
    1922; The Homosexual Neurosis, Boston,
    1922. (Reprints Emerson, NYC 1936).

(68)

A Closing Note

It is fairly certain that no one who reads this book
will fail to find something—and probably many things—
with which he (or she) disagrees, meekly or violently.

The very nature of the material makes any dogmatic
finality impossible. Many definitions and concepts
are subject to different impressions and
interpretations. Words, phrases and places are
constantly passing out of circulation and being
replaced by new words, phrases and places. Today's
realities are tomorrow's memories.

The authors contemplate future editions and will be
very happy to receive suggestions and editorial
information of any sort for correction or addition in
future editions. You can pass your suggestions back
along the same route through which you received this
booklet.

(69)

Gay Girl's Guide
to
New York

Everything from the Plaza to the Pines

A Joint Project Of:
The Sodomite Chamber of Commerce,
The American Pollatelic Society,
Seminal Vampires of America, Inc.
Svasarnt Nerf, Editor

Second Edition
(Summer, 1950)

Gay Girl's Guide
to
New York

Second Edition
(Summer, 1950)

Excerpts

Roof, Coney Island Baths

THE FELLATORIUM

Everard's Turkish Baths, occupying a site successively that
of a Greek Orthodox Church and a Brewery, continues to play a
major role in New Sodom's gay life.

The Golden Age of 1947-49* has become a thing of the past,
thanks to the employment of private police to patrol the area.
Despite this, and with the cost remaining as high as ever
($2.75/$3.50), on weekend nights there is a long line of waiters
for rooms and often enough for dormitory space. There is also
some activity on weekday nights, when the cost is only 50 cents
less.

The major dormitory space and traditional center of things
is on the 2nd floor (an inactive dormitory is on the 1st floor).
There are some private rooms on this floor, but most are on the
3rd Floor. Below the main floor,

*See 1949 Edition

(24)

THE FELLATORIUM

which contains only the lockers, a restaurant and the inactive
dormitory, are found the steam room, showers and swimming
pool, the use of any of which seems to surprise and annoy the
attendants.

Because of continuous inspections of the big 2nd Floor
dormitory by the guards, the old daisy-chains and mass
exhibitions are only memories. For the most part, sex is very
brief and furtive.

According to the ritual, if the guard catches two in the
act, the cock-suckee is completely ignored; the cock-sucker is
obliged to give his locker number and is expected to dress and
to leave the premises shortly, and never darken the door
again—at least for 24 hours. As might be expected, the tempo
of the scrutiny increases in proportion to the size of the
waiting line of cash customers.

There is no attempt to exercise

(25)

control over doings in the private rooms and hence their possessors are more valued than ever. Accordingly, all of the 2nd Floor queens proceed to cruise on the 3rd Floor, which is contrary to the rules, but not a "capital" offense when detected, and rarely resulting in expulsion from the baths—only from the 3rd Floor.

It is of course very surprising that in spite of the hypocrisy and insolence of the owners and guards, Everard's continues as popular as ever. The most obvious explanation is the lack of any real competition. While there are many other baths in NYC, none can compare with even the Reformed Everard's.

(26)

Roof, Coney Island Baths

Gay Girl's Guide
to
The U.S. & The Western World

2nd Edition
Summer, 1950

A Primer for Novices
A Review for Roués
An Encyclopedia for All

SWASARNT NERF
Vice-Pres., Seminal Vampires of America

MOIRA ROUSSEDAIQUE
Prof. of French & Clitorology, Gomorrah U.

A Phallus Press Publication

Gay Girl's Guide
to
The U.S. & The Western World

2nd Edition

Summer, 1950

Excerpts

Atlantic City

Girl:

This booklet has been procured for you through the kindness of
your dear mother, or perhaps, your dear sister.

In presenting it to you, she hopes that you will make the fullest
possible use of it to develop all your talents and to get the
most out of life.

Because of the survival of various archaic laws, it might be just
as well if you didn't leave it around to be studied   by your
mother (the other one), your landlady, your Sgt. or your CPO, as
the case may be.

If the envelope wears out, try to get another one. If you can't,
at least keep a pair of rubber bands around it.

Be careful who you show it to. A wrong decision would have
unfortunate results not only for you but for a few million others
besides.

(1)

The Traymore Hotel in Atlantic City
(Demolished in 1972)

Atlantic City

Gay Girl's Guide

to

The U.S. & The Western World

3rd Edition
Mid-50s

SWASARHE MERF
Vice-Pres., Seminal Vampires of America
Cruising Editor of The Queen's Gazette

HONRI HOUSSEDMIQUE
Prof. of French & Clitorology, Gomorrah U.

P. DOE MINIK
Author, "Boys Are Such Dolls"
    "The Problem of Bisexuality:
        Boys vs. Young Men"

Gay Girl's Guide
to
The U.S. & The Western World

3rd Edition
Mid-50s

Excerpts

112

VENEREAL DISEASE

Homosexuals are subject to both Gonorrhea and Syphilis.
Both are curable by the same drug--penicillin, the shots varying
from 1 to 20, at a cost of around $6 each. (In some cities there
are free Public Health Centers; however, they require more
questions and waste of time than a private doctor but even he
must report it.)

The Clap shows up 3 to 7 days after contact and being
obvious and painful is rarely allowed to go beyond its primary
stage--a swollen penis. 1 to 3 shots will cure it at this stage.
If not then treated, it will go away there and spread to other
internal organs, requiring in later years operations, if not
cured in the meantime, in this secondary stage, by many shots of
penicillin. The source of infection can only be anal and not
oral.

You may also unwittingly get into this secondary stage by
being browned by an infected one (before he notices being
infected, say 48 hours after his contact)

(22)

VD

Feeling no ill-effects, you become a "Typhoid Mary" until
told by a victim. As already mentioned, cure in this stage
requires several times as many shots as in the primary stage.

Syphilis is in every way more complex and dangerous. It
can be gotten from an infected penis entering upstairs or
downstairs (only rarely from spit, an open rash or an object with
the germs on). The first sign, after about 3 weeks, is the small
chancre. If on the penis it is usually noted but in the mouth or
ass may not be. Inexplicable hoarseness and stiffness also shows
up at this stage, when 5 to 10 shots will cure.

If not treated, a rash a couple of weeks later indicates
the secondary stage. Its heaviest concentration is usually near
where the chancre was. A sore throat and fever follows.
Treatment now takes 10 to 20 shots. If not treated, the symptoms
disappear in about a month.

(23)

For anyone dumb enough to allow it to go into the tertiary stage (which may take decades to come) the signs are clusters of rashes on the arms, palms and legs and a drooping eyelid. It is then that insanity, various forms of paralysis etc. come and how much good penicillin could still do doesn't seem too well established.

A free and easy way to find out if you have syphilis (assuming there are indications but without the obvious phallic chancre) is to offer a blood donation. You blood is first subject to a Wasserman test before it goes into the blood bank. Naturally, you'll be told fast enough if it's "positive".

The Wasserman test indicates not the germs themselves but the antibodies formed by your blood against them. For about six months after shots have essentially cured you, the Wasserman remains "positive" (but with the concentration or "titre" diminishing). During this period, tests every month or few months continue to provide an expense.

(24)

Alone in a Crowd

Where to Make Contacts

PARKS & PUBLIC PLACES—U.S.

　　The park or square forms the basic gay rendezvous in every city. It can　often be located merely by logical deduction, and through contacts made there, can provide the key to other phases of gay life in the town. Parks are more or less unchanging from year to year and can be little affected by police pressure or even raids.

　　The park or square is usually a smallish one, not far from the center of town, with one particular side, area or lane most popular.

　　For your convenience, some of the leading spots of this sort in the U.S. and Abroad follow.

　　Included also are some miscellaneous public places—Streets, T-rooms of the public, rail or bus variety, the latter abbreviated GBD for Greyhound Bus Depot.

(30)

PARKS & PUBLIC PLACES—U.S.

Atlanta:　Piedmont Park; Grant Park

Boston:　Botanical Gardens nr. Beacon St.

Chicago: Boardwalk between Oak & Division
Cincinatti: Lyttle Park; Fountain Square;
　　　　　　Eden Pk.; Burnett Woods near
　　　　　　Clifton St.; GBD
Cleveland:　Wade Park
Columbus:　Goodale Park; Capitol Grounds

Detroit:　Grand Circus Park; GBD

Huntington:　Court House Sq.; Ritter Park

Indianapolis:　American Legion Pk (e. side)

Los Angeles:　Pershing Square (eastern arm)

Miami:　Bayfront Park (southern half)
Minneapolis:　Loring Park

(31)

PARKS & PUBLIC PLACES—U.S.

New York: Bryant Park, eastern arm
            Central Park, e. of 78th & CPW
                  "   " , e. of 69th & CPW
            CPW benches betw. 68th & 79th
            Riverside Pk betw. 72nd & 79th
            Soldiers and Sailors Monument
            3rd Ave. betw. 45th & 55th Sts.
            42nd St. betw. 7th & 8th Aves.
            T-Rooms of Grand Central; Times
            Sq. subway (3), IRT 72nd & 116th
            and Columbus Circle (3) Subway

New Orleans: Jackson Square

Omaha: Bayliss Pk; 18th & Farnum; GBD

Philadelphia: Rittenhouse Square

San Francisco: Union Square
St. Louis: Forrest Pk (nr Audubon &
                          Kingshighway)
Seattle: Woodland Park

Washington: Lafayette Park; GBD

(32)

PARKS AND PUBLIC PLACES—ABROAD

Amsterdam: Rembrandt Square

Brussels: Place Brouckere & T-room

Copenhagen: Tivoli area

Hague: Buitenhof Square

Hamburg: T-room outside Bahnhof

London: Hyde Park corner
         Marble Arch
         Leicester Square
         Picadilly Circus

Paris: Avenue Gabrielle; T-room near
        Rue Washington

Rome: Colosseum ruins

(33)

MOVIE THEATERS

Atlanta: Paramount; Grand
Boston: Orpheum; Art; Trans-Lux
Chicago: McVickers; Oriental; Clark;
   Englewood: Ace; Empress; Linden;
             Stratford
Cincinnati: Lyric; Grand
Cleveland: Embassy
Columbus: Broad; Southern; Uptown
Detroit: Colonial; Fox; Times Square
Indianapolis: Circle; Lyric; Loew's
Kansas City: Esquire; Regent; Tower
L.A.: Golden Gate; Music Hall
   Hollywood: Grauman's Egyptian Theater
Louisville: Ohio; Kentucky
Memphis: Princess

(35)

MOVIES

Minneapolis: Astor; Crystal; Palace
New Orleans: Lyceum; Strand
New York: Pix; Bryant; Selwyn; New
           Amsterdam (et al. on 42nd)
           Trans-Lux Colony; Beacon;
           Riverside; 68th St Playhouse
Omaha: Omaha; State
Philadelphia: Family
Pittsburgh: Barry; State
San Francisco: Portola; State
St. Louis: Carrick; Lyric; Senate
Seattle: Colonial; Florence; Winter
         Garden
Toledo: Granada; Rivoli
Washington: Hippodrome; Metropolitan

(Abroad movie theaters are rendered
 useless by excess of attendants.)

(36)

BARS

Albany: Skipper's
    Asbury Park: Fox's
    Atlanta: Vocalis; 5 O'Clock; Club 56
    Atlantic City: McCrory's; 500

    Boston: Punch Bowl; Napoleon Club;
              Chess Room; Silver Dollar
    Buffalo: 5 O'Clock; Carousel; Ryan's;
              Pat's; Versailles Room

    Chicago: Lake Shore; Dunes; Shoreline
              Seven; Dome (Sherman Hotel)
    Cincinnati: Club Melody; Hangar;
                Cricket
    Columbus, O.: Frolics

    Dallas: Reno; Gypsy; Music Box

(38)

120

BARS

Dayton: Kitty Hawk Room
Denver: Tic-Tac; Ship's Tavern
Detroit: Palais; La Rosa's; Rio Grande

El Paso: Green Tree; Green Frog

Hartford: Crown Oyster Bar; Corky's;
          Houblein's
Houston: Pink Elephant; Tonga
Huntington: Martin's Grill; Nasser

Indianapolis: Brass Rail; Mirror Room

Jacksonville: Fletcher's

Kansas City: Omar Room (Continental)

Lexington: Zebra; Golden Horseshoe
Little Rock: Brass Rail
Long Beach, Calif.: Rendezvous Club

(39)

BARS—U.S.

Los Angeles: Maxwell's; Crown Jewel;
              Earl Hotel
 Hollywood: Golden Carp; Circle;
             House of Ivy
Louisville: Gordon's; Beaux-Arts

Memphis: Creel Room (Peabody)
Miami: Alibi; Gibson's; Duffy's Tavern;
        Mozaluna; Leon & Eddie's;
        Moulin Rouge
  Miami Beach: Circus; Club Benny's
Milwaukee: Dome; Curley's; Andrews H.
Monterrey: Pigalle; Oasis; Host

Nashville: Hermitage Hotel
New Haven: La Couronne; Kasey's; Taft H.
New Orleans: Tony Barcino's Starlet;
              Dixie Bar of Music;
              Lafitte's Garage Bar;
              Roosevelt Hotel

(40)

BARS—U.S.

New York:
  Midtown: Silver Rail; Club 44 (Terrace)
                 Café 43 (Town); Arty's; Rivi-
                 era; Bernard's; Faisan d'Or
  East Side: Blue Parrot; Shaw's; Bob's
                 Intermezzo; Lodge; East 55
    Village: Mary's; Old Colony; Main St.;
                 Club 31; Old Place (D)
  Lower East: Capri (dancing)
  West Side: Cork
  Long Island: West Park Inn, Hempstead
Norfolk: Lynd Haven

Oakland: Pearl's
Omaha: Frolics; Seven Seas

Paterson: Adele's; Sunny Point
Philadelphia: Maxine's; Surf; Pirate
              Ship; Forrest Theater Bar
Pittsburgh: Horseshoe Bar

Portland, Ore.: Music Hall

(41)

122

Providence: Silver Dollar
Provincetown: Atlantic; Wuthering Heights
Roanoke: Trade Winds
Rochester: Seneca Hotel
St. Louis: Entre-Nous; Uncle Joe's;
            Al's; Flamingo; Gaslight
  E. St. Louis: English Inn
St. Paul: Drum
Frisco: Seven Seas; Jim Dolan's; Sea
         Cow; Ethel's; 181; 585; Paper
         Doll; Gordon's; Keno

Santa Fé: La Fonda Hotel
Seattle: Snake Pit; Garden of Allah
Washington: Chicken Hut; Chuck's; Sand's

(42)

BARS—ABROAD

British Isles
   Bristol: White Elephant
   Dublin: Davy's; Dawson's
   Edinburgh: Royal British; County;
               Waterloo; Ivanhoe
   Glasgow: Lauderdale
   London: White Room; Fitzroy's; Irish
           House; George & Dragon; Scott's;
           Queen's Head
 Canada
   Montreal: Mt. Royale Hotel Bar;
              Pool's; Tropicale
   Toronto: Beverage Room; Ford;
             Savarin
 Hawaii
   Honolulu: Tropics; Wagon Wheel;
              Waikiki Tavern
 Mexico
   Mexico City: Ritz Hotel
 South Africa:
   Johannesburg: Rudolf's Attic & Rudolf's
                                 Cellar

(43)

Western Europe

```
Amsterdam:  Rigo;  Nol;  Jamaica Inn
Berlin:     Barth;  Kleist;  Telfi Palast;
            Hütte;  Gerda Kelch;  Fürstenau
            Bier-Bar;  Berliner Kind'l
Berne:      Selim's
Bremen:     Bremer Schlüssel
            Hanseatenstübchen
Brussels:   Monte Christo;  Cabano
Cannes:     Zanzi-Bar;  Casanova;  Petit Trou
            Costa Rica;  Les Trois Cloches
Copenhagen: Bollman's Kellar;  Admiral
            Krugo;  Captain's Bar;
            Dragvig's Bodega
Duisberg:   Amourette
Düsseldorf: Hünnenstübchen
```

(44)

```
Frankfort:  Petit Moulin Rouge;  Kolibri;
            Mainterrasse;  Rote Katz;
            Santos;  Teddy's;  Folsonkeller
Genoa:  Beri-Beri
Hague:  Van Regina;  Donnehut;  Corona
Hamburg:  Bronzekeller;  Theaterklause;
          Roxi;  Stadt Casino;  Oaso;
          Bar-Colona;  Monocle;  Tante Erna;
          Lorelei;  Tabasco;  Davidsklause
Hanover:  Zur Schlossklause
Heidelberg:  Nach Acht
Milan:  Piccolo;  Gatto Verde;  Carminati
Munich:  Dultstube;  Spinne
Nurnberg/Fürth:  Sechsamstube
Paris:  Equinox;  Festival;  Carousel;  Mars
        Coup de Frein;  Boeuf-sur-le-Toit
Rome:  Rupo Torpeio;  Riccardo's
```

(45)

BARS; FRATS

Stockholm: Regenbogen; Umbrella
              Excelsior Hotel

Stuttgart: Doblstube; Gymnasium;
              Hoptonblüte

Turin: Alemagni; Washington

Venice: Grotto

Zurich: Blauen Himmel; Java; Mary's

Fraternities/Sororities

There is a current movement to spread throughout the land local
chapters of the Mattachine Society, based on the European-type
fraternal organizations. For information on your local set-up,
write:

    The Mattachine Society
    P.O. Box 1925
    Main Post Office
    Los Angeles 53, Calif.

(46)

126

LITERATURE

III Periodicals
    A. Homosexual magazines (in the
       nature of "trade journals")

            In English
                One magazine. 232 S. Hill St.
                                Los Angeles 12
            In German
                Der Kreis, Postfach 547, Zurich 22
                Die Gefahrten, Arndstrasse 3
                                Frankfurt
                Der Weg, Colonnadenstrasse 5
                        Hamburg 36, Germany
                Hellas, Neustadtstrasse 48
                        Hamburg 36, Germany
            In Danish
                Vennen, Postbox 809, Copenhagen

                        (67)

                LITERATURE—Periodicals

            In French
                Arcadie, Rue Jeanne-d'Arc 162
                                Paris, France
                Futur, Rue de Clichy 57, Paris
            In Italian
                Sesso o Liberta, Bal. Partigi-
                        ani 3, Novara, Italy
            In Dutch
                Vriendschap, P.O. Box 542
                                Amsterdam

    B. Magazines with pin-ups & models etc.

        Physique Pictorial, 1834 W. 11ᵗʰ, LA
        Tomorrow's Man, 22 E. Van Buren, Chgo
        Männer im Bild, V. Rolf Putziger
                Colonnadenstr. 5, Hamburg 36
            (many others of less eminence)

                        (68)

128

PICTURES

Most of the following offer all photographic varieties--black-and-white prints large and small, color prints,   color slides, and, in a few cases, movies. Very few are complete nudes and none "in sex". (Quaintance has drawings.)

U.S.

Athletic Model Guild, 1834 W. 11th St
Los Angeles 6
California Models, 3337 Tombrook Dr.
Sacramento 21
Spectrum Films, 18924 Vine St.
Cincinnati, 10
George Quaintance, Box 192, Phoenix
Lon Studios, 400 W. 57th, N.Y. 19

Europe

International Modelfoto Service
P.O. 330 Copenhagen V
V. Rolf Putziger c/o Der Weg (see p. 67)
V. Schmidt c/o Hellas (see p. 67)

(69)

Passing a Joint

130

Riis Beach in the 'Sixties

A Photo Essay

   During the 1960s, a large number of gay visitors migrated
to a remote section of Riis Beach in Queens, and at some point
clothing came to be optional. This lasted until 1972, when Jacob
Riis Park was turned over to the National Park Service and
rangers began issuing tickets.

The following snapshots were made by Richard P. on those
brilliant summer days of the 'sixties.

146

Vintage Porn

A Photo Essay

These undated pictures include some images which evidently circulated as prints. Other items include some contact sheets and glossies with crop markings. Finally it also has some fading images made with the Polaroid Land Camera, which developed photos (almost) instantly—you did not have to take a roll of film to a developer to have prints made (which might be seen by unsympathetic viewers).

A Sepia Print

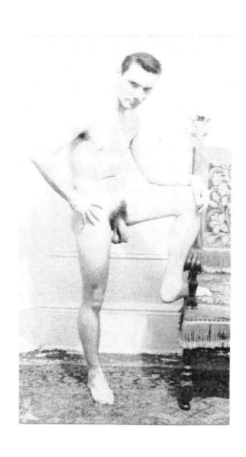

Shore Leave

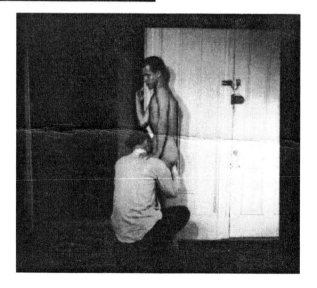

The Busy Fluffer

Scenes from a Contact Print

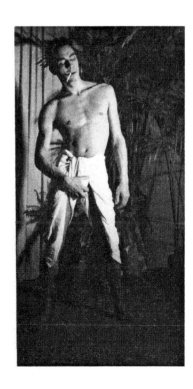

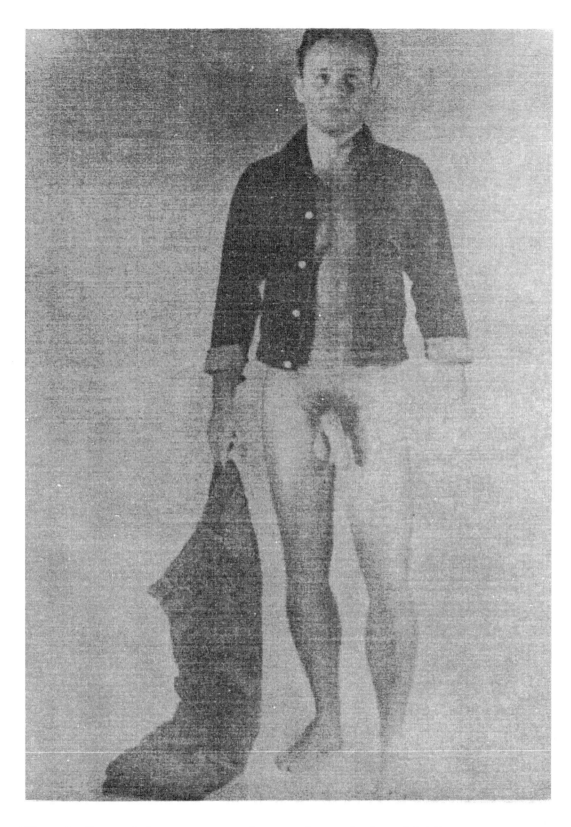

The Polaroid camera, introduced in 1947, provided
instant gratification.

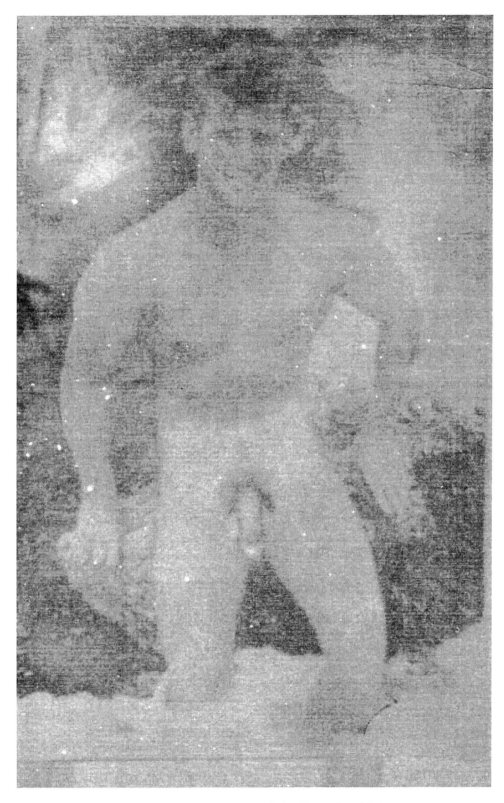

Instant, but swiftly fading.

TROJAN

MALE NUDISTS
PLAYING CARDS
© 1966 CENTRAL SALES

1959

1961—Tom of Finland

ACME

BODY BEAUTIFUL

50c
U.K. 3/6

STUDIES IN MASCULINE ART

1961

ACME

men

AND

art

VOLUME 11   50¢

joe bongi

1962

Happy New Year, 1963!

THE YOUNG PHYSIQUE

NOVEMBER / TWO DOLLARS

1963

beach adonis MAY 75¢ K

1966

Trojan Male Nudist Playing Cards

1966

The Grecian Guild, founded in 1955 by Henry L. Womack, was the main publisher-distributor of gay books and magazines in the U.S.

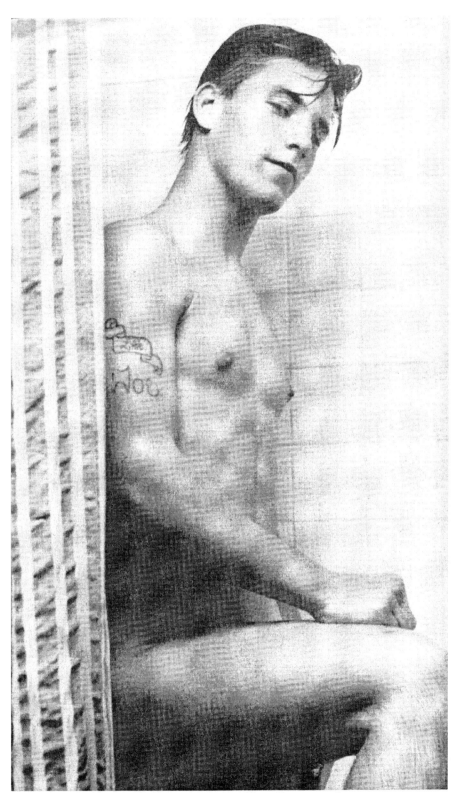

Joe Dallessandro appeared in the May
1967 issue of Grecian Guild Pictorial,
just 18 and about to be discovered by
Andy Warhol and Paul Morrissey.

MODERN MALE

ACME
Collectors Edition
$1.50

VOLUME ONE

8 MAGNIFICENT COLOR PAGES

TOR LIND
(Swede)

PHOTO ART OF TODAY'S GREAT YOUNG PHYSIQUES

1968—The editors have thoughtfully supplied a
swimsuit with pen and ink.

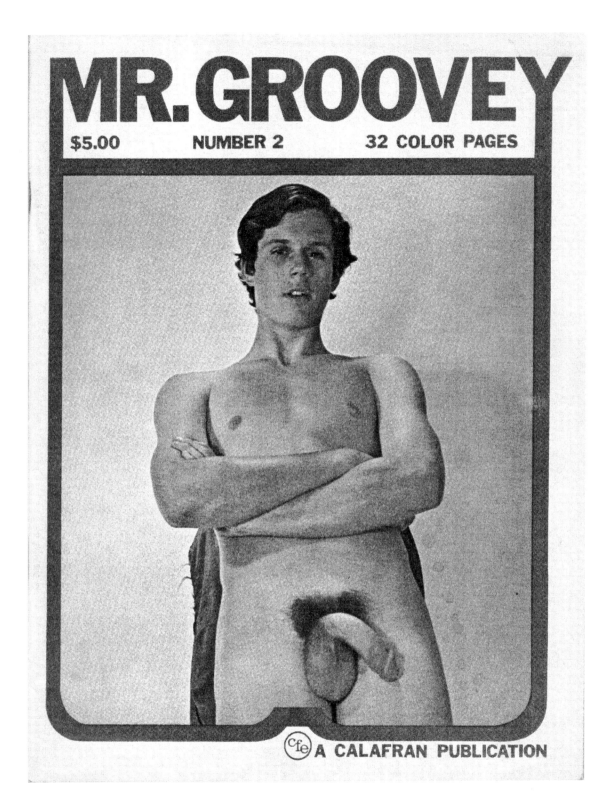

1969—Mr. Groovey, ready for Woodstock and Stonewall.

The Lady Jai Recommended List (1954)

When I was finishing the first (2004) edition of *The Gay Guides for 1949*, I heard from Tim Retzloff about research he was doing on pre-Stonewall gay guides, including the Lady Jai list from 1954.

Tim kindly sent me a copy, and a letter which said:

You asked for more information about Lady Jai. Enclosed is a photocopy of his "Recommended List," compiled, according to its author, around 1954. Lady Jai, who was secretary of the Detroit Area Council of the MattachineSociety during its short existence from 1958 to 1960, mimeographed the listing for a network of friends who traveled for the auto industry. Alas, I fear the original is now lost, since its owner, Detroit Mattachine chairman Hal Lawson, died earlier this year.

Lady Jai's straight name was J.A. Moore, and at that time he was living in St. Petersburg.

Tim Ratzloff has contributed a great number of articles for periodicals and books on queer history in the U.S., especially in Michigan, with special attention to the role of the automobile in the history of sexual liberation.

Lady Jai's list was two pages of single-spaced typewriting on paper of 8 ½ by 14 inches. For this publication I have cut-and-pasted them into three pages. They cover 26 states plus Canada, and one listing each for Nogales, Mexico; Bogotá; and Tokyo.

THE LADY JAI RECOMMENDED LIST

(Bistros and Spas, gathering spots for Le Crowd Gay)

*-"All the way"   S- "Semi"

ARIZONA
Yuma- Flamingo Court

CALIFORNIA
Hollywood: Allegro Club,
The Interlude, Flamingo Club,
The Circle, Gayla Club
Laguna Beach: Los Ondas
La Jolla: Morries
Long Beach: The Commodore,
The 557, The Holler Inn
Los Angeles: The Crown Jewel,
Waldorf Cellar, Le Beau Club,
Tropical Village, Santessus
Club, The Captains Room,
Maxwells. San Diego: The 1202,
Copacabana, Smittys Cafe, The
Peacock. San Francisco: 509 Club,
Finnochios (Drag), Silver Dollar,
Silver Rail, Kenos Bar*, Black Cat
The Beige Room (Drag), Paper Doll,
Dolans, The 181 Club.

COLORADO   Denver: The Steak Bar.

DISTRICT OF COLUMBIA Washington:
Chicken Hut*, Carrols, Deauville,
Harrington Hotel Bar, Jewel Box*

FLORIDA   Clearwater: The Stardust.
Miami: Connies Hideaway, Alibi*,
Latin-American, Leon & Eddies,
Singing Bar, Moulin Rouge, Ship-
Deck,* Jewel Box
Miami Beach: Delicate Frank Club,
Club Echo, Duffy's Tavern.
Palm Beach: Capitol Lounge, Melody
Club* Pensacola: San Carlos Bar,
Sir Gays, Trader Johns.
St.Petersburg: The Crystal
Tampa: Fingies, Knotty Pine,
Hillsborough Hotel Bar.

GEORGIA   Atlanta: The Lounge,
Peachtree Lounge, Zebra Lounge,
The Dominoe, Mrs. P's* Picalo Lounge,
Camelia Gardens, Mammy's Shanty
Augusta: Tap Spot. Columbus: The
Office Bar-Waverly Hotel, Hidden Door,
The Open Door. Savannah: Sapphire Room*

(NOTE: It must be noted that Gay Bars
fluctuate constantly, as to
ownership, "reception," locale,
clientele, general conditions
etc. This list is a compila-
tion from many sources. We try
to keep it up to date, but very
often this is not possible.
Good luck!)

Illinois Chicago: (These change
names and fluctuate constantly!)
The Storm, Omars* 509 Club,
Town and Country-S(in the Palmer
House, College of Complexes-S
The Dome (Hotel Sherman)-S, Haig,
Shore Line Seven*, Sames*
(Suburban): LOU GAGES*
The 1429- Clark Street

KANSAS Kansas City: Omar Room-S
The Terrace Lounge, Golden Horse-
Shoe. Wichita: Blue Lantern

KENTUCKY Covington: Jewels.

LOUISIANA Baton Rouge: Lafittes.
Lake Charles: St.Regis Bar
New Iberia: Bob's Bar, Monroe:
Monroe Hotel Bar, Alvis Hotel.
New Orleans: Dixies, Rendousvous
My-O-My Bar, Starlit Roof (Drag)
Lafittes in Exile, Driftwood*
Tony Baccinos, Sams Village Bar,
The Golden Rod, Penguin, Ivans.
Shreveport: Bill & Toms.

MARYLAND Baltimore: Diamond Back
Lounge*, Martins Bar, Pauls Bar,
Silver Dollar.

MASSACHUSETTS Boston: Chess Room-
Hotel Touraine, Statler Bar(Natch)
Punch Bowl* Napoleon*, Silver
Dollar,* Playland-21 Essex, Marios
Jacques-77 Charles Street
CAPE COD: PROVINCETOWN: The Moors,
Sea Dragon, Atlantic House Bar,
Ace of Spades, The Town House,
Phil Bayon's Weathering Heights
(All Gay - Bars, cafes, town,
environs etc.)

MICHIGAN DETROIT: The 1011 (Rio
Grande Bar, 1011 FarmerSt.)
La Rosas, Silver Dollar, Royal,
Palais, The Golden Slipper, Blue
Crest, Diplomat, Woodward Lounge
(All open-gay) Following are
Semi-Gay: Silver Star, Hotel
Statler Bar (Natch!) Men's Bar at
The Sheraton Hotel(Parade Bar)
Stage Door, Brass Rails-Adams &
The Boulevard & Woodward, Rheumes
Restaurant at the Blvd & Woodward
Hub Grill, Seros Restaurant-after
2:00. Detroit-Wayne Baths.-Wild!

MINNESOTA Minneapolis:
Herb's Bar, Curley's Night
Club(the Bar),Minneapolis Bar
St.Paul: Kirmser Bar

MISSISSIPPI Biloxi: Buena Vista
Hotel Bar, Aquarium Bar
Jackson: The Cellar Bar

MISSOURI Kansas City:Jewel Box.
St.Louis: Georges, Uncle Johns,
Flamingo Room, Steeplechase.

NEW JERSEY Atlantic City: Madrid
Club, Entertainers Club* West-
minster Alley Club, McCrary Lounge,
Brighton Cocktail Lounge, Jockey

NEW YORK Albany: Ten-Eyke Hotel Bar
Buffalo: Alibi, Glass Bar, Ryans*
Oasis* Johnny's Club 68*
NEW YORK CITY: (All Gay or Semi)
There are approximately 72 Gay Bars
in the New York City area. We list
but a few.) Arties-45th off Brdwy
Faison D'Or, Town Bar, Plaza Bar,
Larry's Bar, Club Capri (Drag) East
Five Five (55th & 3rd) Golden Dollar,
Regent's Row (58th & 1st) Hotel Astor
Bar- Much Elegant, Tony's Lodge, The
Deauville, Intermezzo (Lexington, Movies
Tues. eve.) Jilly's Bar, Saw Dust Trail,
Martins Bar, Reveria Lounge, Builders
Bar, Terrace Lounge (44th & 6th)
Charlies Bar, La Chandelle Lounge,
Wishbone (58th & 7th), Sans Souci,
The Blue Angel-Bar, Park West.
The Village: Bon Soir, Marys (W.14th)
Main Street, The Moroccan Village,
Tony Pastors-Bar, Monas Bar, One Fifth
Ave, 181 Club (2nd Ave) Lennies.

NORTH CAROLINA: Ashville- Sky Club,
Highlands: Helens Barn, Rats Nest.

NORTH DAKOTA: Grand Forks: Hotel
Grand Forks- Bar.

OHIO   Akron- Lincoln. Cincinnati:
Cricket-Bar, Key Hole Club, Melody Bar*
The 10-0-5, Wiggens Bar. Cleveland:
Cadillac Lounge (Much elegant...?)
ORCHID (12th & Walnut). Zanzibar.
For Health fans: The Ohio Health Inst.
Columbus: The Blue Feather.
Dayton: Riviera Lounge. Toledo: The
Scenic, La Rue Lounge, Ivanhoe.
Philcoffs.

PENNSYLVANIA   Scranton: Polka Dot,
Philadelphia: New Look Lounge, Green
Dragon, Ferrest Restaurant. Pittsburg:
Carnival, Horseshoe.

TEXAS Dallas: Zila's Band Box*
Blue Bonnet, Holiday,* Night
Bomber, The Horseshoe. Fort
Worth: The Longhorn. Galveston:
Omar Khyhams. Houston: Tonga,
Desert Room, Pink Elephant,
Effies.

VIRGINIA   Richmond: Oriental Cafe.

WASHINGTON   Seattle: Maison Blanc,
Fox & Hounds* Tam-O-Shanter,
Rathskellers Bar, The Captains
Room, Double Header Lounge,
Garden of Allah, Marine Room,
Ivars Acres of Clams, The
Stewart House,Spokane:Marlin Inn

WISCONSIN   Eau Clair: Cameo Room.
La Crosse: Club Flamingo (Carl
& Ruby Kreklow-owners)
Milwaukee: The Forum, Riviera,
The Whitehorse* Royal Hotel Bar,
Celebrity Club. Flame & Faust.

CANADA   Calgary, Alta.-
Pallser Hotel Bar, Edmonton:
MacDonald Hotel Bar
British Columbia: Vancouver-
Castle Hotel,* Vancouver Hotel,
Georgia, Devonshire. Victoria:
Empress Hotel Bar. Winnipeg,
Manitoba: Childs Restaurant,
Marlborough Hotel Parlor* Royal
Alexandria Hotel Parlor, St.
Regis Hotel Parlor, Vendome
Hotel -ditto. Ontario:
Hamilton: Royal Connaught-Bar.
London: Club 400, Silver Dollar.
Niagara Falls: Gen.Brock Hotel.
Ottawa: Canada House Lounge.
Toronto: Nile Room, "Letros"*
Park Plaza Bar, Royal York Hotel,
King Edward Hotel Tavern, Times
Square Bar.* Windsor: St.
Clair Tavern, Killarnie Castle-
Bar, Metrople-Bar, Piccadilly-
Prince Edward Hotel.
Quebec: Tropical Lounge* Peel
Tavern* Eagle Club, Pine Lounge,
Piccadilly Club,* Mnt.Royal
Hotel Tavern* Cafe de la Paix,
Plateau Tavern, Altess Tavern,
42nd Club, Ceinture Fleche,
Indian Room, Maritime Bar.
Quebec City: Capitol Tavern*
Chez Maurice Lounge, Clarendon
Hotel Tavern. St.Johns: Jewel
Box, New Windsor Hotel-Bar.
Sask: Regina: Sask. Hotel Tavern
Saskatoon: Bessborough Hotel Tav.

MEXICO: Nogales: B29 Bar

S. AMERICA: Bogota: Columbia:
The Hacienda Blanco, 11 Calla 421

TOKYO, JAPAN: Peters Bar.

172